D1257272

FENELON'S
DIALOGUES ON ELOQUENCE

FENELON'S

DIALOGUES ON ELOQUENCE

A TRANSLATION

WITH AN INTRODUCTION AND NOTES BY

WILBUR SAMUEL HOWELL

PRINCETON NEW JERSEY

PRINCETON UNIVERSITY PRESS

1951

Publication of this book was aided by a grant
from the Princeton University Research Fund

Printed in the United States of America by Princeton
University Press at Princeton, New Jersey

Title page decoration is from
the first Paris edition of the *Dialogues*.

For my son S. C. H.

CONTENTS

ACKNOWLEDGMENTS

THE University Research Committee of Princeton University made a substantial contribution to the cost of publishing this book. I should like to take this opportunity to thank them for their generosity.

To my colleagues, Professor Ira O. Wade and Professor Whitney J. Oates, who consented to give me criticisms and suggestions as I was preparing this book, I should like to express my appreciation, if I may do so without making them in any way responsible for errors or weaknesses in these pages.

Mr. Datus C. Smith, Jr., Director of the Princeton University Press, has been most courteous and thoughtful in lending me assistance of various kinds. I am grateful to him for his assistance, and to his staff for theirs, among whom Miss Harriet Anderson deserves explicit mention.

I should like especially to thank my wife for everything she did to further this enterprise.

W. S. H.

20 Armour Road
Princeton, New Jersey
July 12, 1950

Introduction

I. SCOPE OF THE *DIALOGUES*

To classify Fénelon's *Dialogues on Eloquence* as a treatise on preaching is to say that the work has a much narrower purpose that its author actually intended. It is true, of course, that Fénelon had pulpit oratory in mind when he wrote it, and that his primary concern was to reformulate the principles of religious eloquence, and thus to improve the preaching of his own day. But it is also true that he did not limit himself to this primary concern. He recognized that preaching is a phase of the larger enterprise of communication, and that any attempt to deal with that phase must be at the same time an attempt to discuss the problems of discourse in general. Thus, without in any way impairing the pragmatic value of his work to the practicing clergyman, he went beyond the sermon, and even beyond the legal and political oration of the layman's world, to survey the entire subject of speaking and writing, and to interest himself in the large outlines of the theory of literary effort. Despite the fact that he probably composed his *Dialogues on Eloquence* at the age of twenty-eight, when he was not yet at home in all the prose forms which he was later to master, his qualifications as a student of the theory of discourse were even then something more than those of a mere youthful novice. His own personal experience as preacher during his early manhood had given him at first hand an understanding of the difficulties involved in bringing the truths of religion within the range of comprehension of the average congregation. His study of Saint Augustine's *De Doctrina Christiana* and of patristic and sacred writings in general had acquainted him with the theory of pulpit rhetoric and with the problems of the religious propagandist. He knew the secular rhetoric of ancient Greece and Rome through his reading of Plato, Aristotle, Cicero, Dionysius of Halicarnassus, Quintilian, and Longinus. These major authorities

1

on communication and persuasion had taught him to perceive the common elements involved in such diverse occupations as those of the teacher of philosophy, the speaker in the court of law, the political leader, the historian, and the writer on science and morality. His sensitive grasp of Homer's *Iliad* and *Odyssey*, of Virgil's *Aeneid*, of the religious poetry of the Bible, and of such doctrinal works as Boileau's *Art of Poetry*, had made him aware of the problems of poetic, as distinguished from rhetorical, communication. His interest in music, painting, and architecture had led him to see the connection among various types of artistic endeavor, and to face the speculative issues that creative effort produces. Thanks to his awareness of these many things, his analysis of the task of the preacher becomes a broad statement of the aims, methods, and standards of authorship in general. As a matter of fact, it is no exaggeration to say that his *Dialogues on Eloquence* are designed to be a complete theory of communication, with primary emphasis upon the preacher and the sermon, and with sustained auxiliary emphasis upon the work of the secular orator, the teacher, the poet, and the artist. His fundamental purpose is to base his theory of preaching upon the theory of art, and to keep everywhere in mind the relations between art and life. Thus his interests are more philosophical than specialized, more humane than technological, more liberal than doctrinaire.

Fénelon's critics have sometimes failed to see that his purpose is to consider preaching not only in itself but also in relation to the other arts of expression. Hence they have praised the literary qualities and the critical insights of some portions of the *Dialogues on Eloquence*, and then have confessed themselves unable to see what bearing those portions have upon the humble occupation of pulpit speaker. For example, in his tribute to this work, Saintsbury applauds Fénelon's condemnation of *des tours de passe-passe*, his excellent passages on Demosthenes, Isocrates, Dionysius of Halicarnassus, and Longinus, his bold attitude towards the question of the perfect hero, his ex-

2

altation of "portraying," of bringing the visual image home to the reader, his scorn of mere verbal fault-finding, and his ardent panegyric on the literary greatness of the Bible and of the Fathers; but, adds Saintsbury, "all these passages, which are almost pure gold of criticism, have nothing special to do with the mere *métier* of the preacher."[1] If these passages have nothing special to do with the mere *métier* of the preacher, Fénelon would stand convicted of having introduced them as shining irrelevancies, and preaching, as a verbal enterprise, would of course have no concern with the issues raised in literary and artistic effort. Neither of these inferences is supported by a study of the *Dialogues on Eloquence*. The passages admired by Saintsbury are an integral part of Fénelon's conception of the special occupation of the preacher; and preaching itself, in his view, is distinguished from other verbal enterprises, not as base metal from gold, but as gold in one shape from gold in another.

II. THE CAST OF CHARACTERS

IN presenting his theory of eloquence in the form of a dialogue, Fénelon is obviously following as literary models the dialogues of Plato and Cicero. The works of the former to which he refers at greatest length are *Gorgias*, *Phaedrus*, and the *Republic*, where Socrates is made to analyze such things as oratory and poetry, art and morality, politics and psychology, in conversation with sophists and men of affairs. The chief source of Fénelon's knowledge of Cicero's rhetorical theory is *De Oratore*, a dialogue between two Roman orators, Antonius and Crassus, with other orators in minor roles. Fénelon's indebtedness to Plato and Cicero is explicitly acknowledged in the course of the conversation

[1] G. Saintsbury, *A History of Criticism and Literary Taste in Europe*, 3 vols., London, 1900-1904, vol. 2, pp. 305-6.

For Fénelon's treatment of the six points mentioned seriatim in Saintsbury's tribute, see below as follows: for the first point, p. 61; for the second, pp. 62-65, 109, 115-117; for the third, pp. 74-75; for the fourth, pp. 92-96; for the fifth, pp. 107-111, 146; for the sixth, pp. 122-133, 138-139, 143-148.

between his three agents; and his use of the dialogue-form may be considered an added compliment to these two authorities. Moreover, the dialogue-form, with its machinery for presenting ideas through fictitious speakers, who take sides, dispute, concede, and at length agree, keeps the author's personality in the background of the reader's consciousness, and other personalities and ideas in the foreground; and so it permits a greater liveliness of presentation, more freedom in treating delicate issues, and more suggestiveness in developing a final point of view, than would a direct type of address.

Thus we can say that the dialogue-form, far from being unfavorable to Fénelon's purpose, as Janet declares it to be,[2] is in fact highly favorable. Furthermore, it is not just to Fénelon to accept Janet's attendant judgment that the three personages of the *Dialogues*, who are designated as *A*, *B*, and *C*, remain cold and colorless anonyms, *C* being almost completely useless, *B* a naïf astonished at everything and *A* the long-winded soliloquizer who monopolizes the stage, and who would have been more interesting had he in reality spoken quite alone. The fact is that Fénelon succeeds in giving each of his agents a distinct individuality and a real share in the discussion. *B*, a young preacher, is pictured as a person who wants not only to improve his own speaking but also to follow the fashions of his day—to get on in the world by dazzling elite congregations with his wit, his skill, his paradoxes, his bright turns of phrase. Thus he admires the ingenuity of an Ash Wednesday sermon he has just heard; and he is prevailed upon by *A* and *C* to describe its "beauties." This situation, with which the present work begins, is a close parallel of that in Plato's *Phaedrus*, where the young Phaedrus opens a conversation with Socrates by admiring and at length reading an ingenious but empty speech of the Athenian orator Lysias. *B*'s view of eloquence is not naive. On the contrary, it is a view widely

[2] P. Janet, *Fénelon*, Paris, 1892, pp. 175-76. A recent French study of Fénelon is less hostile to the *Dialogues* than is Janet. See E. Carcassonne, *Fénelon l'homme et l'œuvre*, Paris, 1946, pp. 16-17, 109.

4

held at the time when Fénelon wrote, as we shall see later. It is against this view that *A* levels his criticism. He believes in rhetoric as a social instrument, not as an instrument of a speaker's personal ambition. He believes that art should call attention to its subject rather than its method—to life rather than to mannerism. He believes that, as Isocrates had earned the displeasure of Aristotle by carrying eloquence from the sphere of work and use into the sphere of amusement and ostentation (see below, p. 117), so should all descendants of Isocrates earn the displeasure of the descendants of Aristotle. *C* takes part in the *Dialogues* as an ally of *A*. Of the 150 speeches of the first dialogue, *C* makes 8, as compared with 73 for *A* and 69 for *B*; and these few serve mainly to underline *A*'s fundamental position. *C* plays a larger part in the second dialogue, where he delivers 17 of the 166 speeches, while *A* makes 81 and *B* 68. Here *C*'s remarks are designed to press *A* into a further explanation of basic terms or to offer support to *A*'s developing theory. In the third dialogue, where 129 speeches are delivered in all, *C* has 47, to 60 for *A* and 22 for *B*. It is at this point that *C* not only develops the portrait of the ideal preacher from the outline previously sketched by *A* (see below, pp. 137-143), but also disagrees for a time with *A* upon the question whether or not man's attempt to use his own eloquence in the effort to convert the world to Christianity is impious in its effrontery and pride (see below, pp. 123-130). This dispute brings out the conclusion that, whereas God's power is alone sufficient to convert the world, and God's word and Christ's example are the sufficient instruments of that power, nevertheless man's eloquence can be prudent or imprudent, its imprudence being shown by a reliance upon subtle human arguments and vain ostentation of language, and its prudence, by a close adherence to the spirit and style of the Gospels. Thus we can hardly say that Fénelon makes *C* a useless and unimportant figure, or *B* a simpleton. Both speakers serve in different ways to develop *A*'s position, and *A* himself does not simply talk on alone.

III. RAMUS, ARNAULD, AND FENELON

WHEN Fénelon constructed the *Dialogues* so as to make Isocrates the symbol of false eloquence, with Plato, Cicero, and Saint Augustine arrayed on the other side, he was not primarily interested in displaying his own classical learning or his personal preference for the best of the ancients as opposed to the best his own times could offer. He was interested rather, as the two preceding sections have intimated, in reforming the literary outlook of the century in which he lived. The ancient controversy between Platonist and sophist had involved the question whether the theory and practice of communication should give primary importance to the need for accuracy of statement, or to the need for pleasing the audience for whom the statement is designed. This question arose as an important consideration in the sixteenth and seventeenth century, and the sophistic answer, which stressed pleasure as the speaker's major aim, achieved a position of ascendancy. If rhetorical theory was to be reformed as a step towards the reform of preaching, the sophistic position had to be attacked. What Fénelon did was to attack this position with weapons forged during the controversy between Plato and the sophists; but it was the desire to win the battle in which he found himself engaged, and not the desire to do homage to those who had fashioned such effective weapons, that governed him in writing the *Dialogues.* He does not mention by name the rhetoricians and teachers who in his own time advocated Isocrates as the model of true eloquence. He does not mention those who were working at his side in the effort to call the orator back from the function of entertainment to the function of persuasion. Even the pulpit orators to whom he alludes as he condemns this or that aspect of seventeenth-century preaching do not readily identify themselves as historical personages, although there can be no doubt that his sharp sketches of them are based upon the prevailing practice of actual preachers.[3] Thus his readers are not given the satis-

[3] See below, p. 98, note 49.

faction of seeing him fully locate his *Dialogues* within his own times or of having him provide unmistakable clues to the identity of his contemporary fellow-workers in the field of preaching and rhetorical theory. But if unmistakable clues are wanting, and some speculation were to be allowed as a substitute, it might be argued that Fénelon's true object of attack in the *Dialogues* is the system of rhetoric taught by Ramus and Talaeus over a hundred years before, and that Fénelon is in reality attempting to reform that system by giving it as broad and as fundamental a revision as Antoine Arnauld had done during Fénelon's boyhood with Ramus' system of dialectic. At any rate, the *Dialogues on Eloquence* contain a view of rhetoric which is not only a thorough repudiation of the teachings of Ramus and Talaeus but is also strikingly analogous to the reforms proposed by Arnauld in his crusade against the logical doctrines of the Ramists. It is to explain the *Dialogues* as one of the aspects of the late seventeenth-century war upon Ramus' neo-scholasticism that the present section is being written.

Peter Ramus, also known by his French name Pierre de la Ramée, occupies an ambiguous position among the intellectuals of the sixteenth century. By his biographers and friendly commentators he is regarded as the most influential philosopher of his time; but he had bitter enemies to contend with while he lived, and later critics to picture him as a pretender in the world of learning.[4] Born in 1515 in the small French village of Cuth, son of a poor laborer, he educated himself in Paris, branded as unauthentic the writings

---

[4] The following works analyze various aspects of Ramus' career and subsequent influence (the list is selective): C. Waddington, *Ramus*, Paris, 1855; F. P. Graves, *Peter Ramus and the Educational Reformation of the Sixteenth Century*, New York, 1912; H. Craig, *The Enchanted Glass*, New York, 1936, pp. 142-59; P. Miller and T. H. Johnson, *The Puritans*, New York, 1938, pp. 28-41, 73-74; P. Miller, *The New England Mind*, New York, 1939, pp. 115-56, 312-30, 493-501; R. Tuve, *Elizabethan and Metaphysical Imagery*, Chicago, 1947, pp. 331-53.

Recent interest in Ramus is not all friendly. See N. E. Nelson, "Peter Ramus and the Confusion of Logic, Rhetoric, and Poetry," *The University of Michigan Contributions in Modern Philology*, No. 2, (April, 1947).

INTRODUCTION

of Aristotle in the examination for his master's degree in arts, acquired great popularity as a teacher in the years that followed, sought thorough reform of the methods then in use to educate students in grammar, rhetoric, and dialectic, was forbidden for a time to lecture in philosophy, thanks to the influence of his enemies, and in the last years of his life was converted to Protestantism only to become one of the victims of the massacre of Saint Bartholomew's Day in August 1572. It is not strange that Ramism, as his doctrines are usually called, should have appealed for the next century not only to a Protestant learning which was deliberately seeking to cultivate itself in the rhetoric and dialectic of reform, but also to a Catholic culture bent upon freeing itself from the oppressive dogmatism of scholastic philosophy. But it would not have pleased Ramus to be known as a Protestant logician or as a foe of Aristotle. He would have denied that his logic had applications for one religious faction that it did not have for another. And, apart from his earlier writings, he seems in general to think that his mission is not only to purify Aristotelian philosophy of all the confusing and redundant materials it had acquired from Aristotle himself and from his subsequent admirers, but also to restate it in its essential outline.

In accomplishing this mission, Ramus made use of three major critical principles. These constitute the very heart of his program of reform, and they are usually called the laws of truth, justice, and wisdom.[5] The law of truth is that any

5 These three laws are stated by Ramus in each one of his major writings. He discusses them in his *Scholarum Grammaticarum Libri XX*, Bk. 1; in his *Scholae Rhetoricae seu Quaestiones Brutinae in Oratorem Ciceronis*, Bks. 9, 11, 15, 16, 17; in his *Scholarum Dialecticarum Libri XX*, Bk. 9; in his *Scholarum Metaphysicarum Libri XIIII*, Bk. 5. These treatises, together with other writings of Ramus, were collected and published as *P. Rami Scholae in Liberales Artes*, Basel, 1569, and the following references are to the three laws as they figure in that volume: *Grammaticae*, column 5; *Rhetoricae*, columns 319-34, 339, 362, 364, 377; *Dialecticae*, columns 311-12, 373-78; *Metaphysicae*, column 916. Ramus also discusses the three laws in one of his Grammatical Prefaces; see *Petri Rami Professoris Regii, & Audomari Talaei Collectaneae Praefationes, Epistolae, Orationes*, Marburg, 1599, pp. 8-11. He also discusses them in the various editions of his famous *Dialecticae Libri Duo*; see *Dialectique de Pierre de la Ramee*, Paris, 1555, pp.

8

statement employed as a principle in any art or science must be universally true—its predicate must be valid for every case comprehended within its subject. The law of justice is that any statement employed as a principle in any art or science must have as predicate the parts that are essential to each other and to the subject. There must be in short a homogeneity from part to part in a scientific statement, and a homogeneity between the statements and their scientific object. The law of wisdom is that any statement employed as a principle in any art or science must be reciprocal. Its subject and predicate, that is, must be interchangeable, one possessing neither more nor less generality than the other. Roland MacIlmaine, the first Briton to edit Ramus' *Dialecticae Libri Duo* and to translate it into English, phrases the three laws thus:

And here we haue three generall documentes to be obserued in all artes and sciences. The first is that all the preceptes and rules shoulde be generall and of necessitie true: and this is called a documente of veritie. The seconde that euery arte be contained within his owne boundes, and witholde nothing appartaining to other artes, and is named a documente of iustice. The third, that euery thing be taught according to his nature, that is: generall thinges, generally: and particuler, particulerly: and this is called a documente of wysdome.[6]

Equipped with these principles, Ramus approached the accumulation of precepts making up the grammatical, rhetorical, dialectical, mathematical, physical, and metaphysical learning of his time. From each of these disciplines in turn he proceeded to strip those materials that seemed under his law of justice to belong more properly to some other subject. At the same time he abandoned altogether in

---

84-85, and *P. Rami Regii Professoris Dialecticae Libri Duo*, Postrema editio post mortem autoris, Paris, 1574, pp. 52-53.

Ramus' interpreters have also featured these three laws as follows: Waddington, *Ramus*, pp. 346-52; Graves, *Peter Ramus*, pp. 110-13; P. A. Duhamel, "The Logic and Rhetoric of Peter Ramus," *Modern Philology*, 46 (February, 1949), pp. 165-71.

6 R. MacIlmaine, *The Logike of the moste Excellent Philosopher P. Ramus Martyr*, Newly translated, and in diuers places corrected, after the mynde of the Author, London, 1574, p. 74.

any discipline those materials that seemed under his law of truth to be ambiguous, uncertain, deceptive in general applicability. Collecting and classifying what had survived these two tests, he sought next under his law of wisdom to reduce the materials of each science to reciprocal propositions, and to put chief propositions together on the highest plane of generality, with lesser propositions arranged on lower planes.

What Ramus did to reform dialectic affords the best possible example of the application of his three principles to the circle of learning of his day. From the training he himself had received in the schools, and from the circumstances of the intellectual life about him, he saw the practice of learned disputation as man's chief instrument in the discovery of truth. He regarded dialectic as the system of concepts which not only regulated and explained disputation, but also could be used in the schools to indoctrinate young men in the high calling of the truth-seeker. His reading of Aristotle's *Topics* and Cicero's *Topics* had taught him that ancient dialectic, as a system of concepts devised to explain disputation, had been organized into two divisions, invention and disposition, or, as we might say today, analysis and synthesis. But, as he well knew from his studies of the rhetorical theories of Aristotle, Cicero, and Quintilian, ancient rhetoric, the system of concepts devised to explain political and legal debate, had an organization which also included the topics of invention and disposition, with style and delivery counted as additional topics, and memory as something that had at least to be mentioned. It seemed clear to Ramus that his law of justice was violated at the point where invention and disposition were claimed both by dialectic and by rhetoric. This law really meant that two arts could not share the same subject matter, and that, when they did, learning was to be accused of an egregious blunder, even as the arts were to be condemned for redundancy and untidiness. As he saw it, he had no recourse but to detach invention and disposition either from the one or the other of the arts which treated them. What he therefore did was to constitute dialectic as the theory of invention and disposition, rhetoric as the theory of style and delivery. Memory, the fifth part of ancient rhetoric, he regarded as a faculty to be assisted and strengthened by what dialectic says on the subject of disposition and method.[7]

In actual fact, Ramus is not the originator of the idea that rhetoric and dialectic should have the constitution just described, nor does he pretend to be. He expressly acknowledges that Sturm's lectures at Paris had shaped his own thinking on dialectic, and he declares Sturm to have been the disciple of Rudolph Agricola.[8] Neither is Ramus to be considered a penetrating critic in accepting the decision that ancient rhetoric and ancient dialectic duplicated each other in treating invention and disposition. Ancient rhetoric, as the theory of communication between the orator and the populace, had a different interest in invention and disposition from that claimed by ancient dialectic, which postulated the learned audience and learned subject matter. The system of invention and disposition assigned to rhetoric in such works as Aristotle's *Rhetoric* and Cicero's *De Inventione* did not duplicate, although it resembled, the system of invention and disposition assigned to dialectic in such works as Aristotle's *Topics* and Cicero's *Topics*.[9] Thus Ramus' program of reform for rhetoric and dialectic

[7] For Ramus' view of the relation between memory and dialectic, see *P. Rami Scholarum Dialecticarum, seu Animadversionum in Organum Aristotelis, libri XX*, Recens emendati per Joan. Piscatorem Argentinensem, Frankfurt, 1581, p. 593. For Talaeus' statement of the Ramist view, see *P. Rami & A. Talaei Collectaneae Praefationes, Epistolae, Orationes*, p. 15.

[8] *P. Rami & A. Talaei Collectaneae Praefationes, Epistolae, Orationes*, p. 67. The Preface in which Ramus acknowledges his indebtedness to Agricola and Sturm belongs to his *De conjungenda eloquentia cum philosophia*. For a discussion of this indebtedness, see Waddington, *Ramus*, pp. 384-85; also Graves, *Peter Ramus*, pp. 17, 98. The more remote antecedents of Ramus' dialectic are given by F. Beurhusius in his *De P. Rami Dialecticae Praecipuis Capitibus Disputationes Scholasticae . . . quae Paedagogiae Logicae Pars Secunda, qua artis veritas exquiritur*, Editio Secunda, London, 1582, pp. 54-68.

[9] The differences between the inventional pattern of ancient rhetoric and that of ancient dialectic are discussed in the present author's *The Rhetoric of Alcuin and Charlemagne*, Princeton, 1941, pp. 33-63.

11

was more tidy than profound, more in the spirit of six-teenth-century humanism than in the spirit of Aristotle and Cicero. But what is important about the program is that it had in Ramus so eloquent a spokesman, so voluminous a writer, and so successful a proselyter, that it seemed to his followers to be wholly original with him and wholly master-ful as a clarification of the ponderous and redundant learn-ing of the scholastic philosophers.

The dialectical system of Ramus is best known in the form which its author gave it in a French version, called *Dialectique*, first published at Paris in 1555, and in a Latin version, called *Dialecticae Libri Duo*, first published in the same city one year later. These two versions, which Ramus intended respectively for his own countrymen and for the learned of other countries, represent by his own admission the labor of twenty years, and the condensing and correcting of his earlier publications on dialectic.[10] One of these earlier publications, *Dialecticae Institutiones*, had first appeared at Paris in 1543 as a treatise without divisions into books or chapters, although it dealt with the subjects of invention and disposition, and contained a full-page table to show all the subdivisions into which Ramus arranges these two sub-jects. By 1552, the *Dialecticae Institutiones* was being pub-lished as a work in three books.[11] Meanwhile, Ramus had published at Paris in 1543 a longer work, *Aristotelicae Ani-madversiones*, which by 1548 had grown into twenty books and later became known as *Scholarum Dialecticarum Libri XX*.[12] It was from these voluminous treatises that Ramus drew the doctrine presented in the *Dialectique* and the *Dia-lecticae Libri Duo*, both of which are divided into only two main parts, and are designed as an epitome of the ancient lore of invention and disposition. Something of the enthu-siasm with which this epitome was received by the disciples

[10] *Dialectique de Pierre de la Ramee*, 1555, Preface.

[11] See Waddington, *Ramus*, pp. 442-43.

[12] It bears this latter title in *P. Rami Scholae in Liberales Artes*, column 1. See also *P. Rami Scholarum Dialecticarum, seu Animadversionum in Organum Aristotelis, libri XX*, Recens emendati per Joan. Piscatorem Argentinensem. See also Waddington, *Ramus*, pp. 444-45, 465.

of Ramus may be seen in the words addressed by Roland
MacIlmaine in 1574 to the readers of his translation of the
Dialecticae Libri Duo. Says he:

As fore the matter whiche it containethe, thou shalt vnderstand
that there is nothing appartayning to dialectike eyther in Aris-
totles XVII. booke [*sic*] of logike, in his eight bookes of Phisike,
or in his XIIII. bookes of Philosophie, in Cicero his bookes of
Oratorie, or in Quintilian (in the which there is almost nothing
that dothe not eyther appartayne to the inuention of argu-
mentes a [*sic*] disposition of the same, but thou shalt fynde it
shortlie and after a perfecte methode in this booke declared.[13]

In his treatment of invention as the first part of dialectic,
Ramus specifies at once that dialectic is the science of disputing well and is to be considered the same science as logic.[14] The phenomenon with which this science deals, he indicates,[15] is the logical proposition. In order for us to make
proper use of disputation, we should know this science, he
declares, "because it proclaims to us the truth of all argument and as a consequence the falsehood, whether the truth
be necessary, as in science, or, as in opinion, contingent, that
is to say, capable both of being and not being."[16] The logical proposition, or argument, as Ramus calls it initially,[17]
has two parts, an antecedent and consequent, or subject and
predicate.[18] Now if we consider how we may analyze the
truth or falsity of one of these propositions, we have to understand that its subject is related to its predicate in one of
ten possible ways: as cause to effect; effect to cause; subject
to adjunct; adjunct to subject; opposite to opposite; like
to like; term to cognate; whole to parts; thing to essence; or,
as the final possibility, subject and predicate are related
arbitrarily by virtue of some outside sanction, as when a
witness testifies that he saw subject and predicate in a certain relation to each other, his testimony being the only
possible way of establishing that relation.[19] Ramus' entire

[13] *Op.cit.*, pp. 7-8.　　　　[14] *Dialectique*, 1555, p. 1.
[15] *Ibid.*, pp. 4-5.　　　　[16] *Ibid.*, p. 2. Translation mine.
[17] *Ibid.*, p. 5.　　　　[18] *Ibid.*, pp. 71-72.
[19] In the *Dialectique*, 1555, Ramus uses the following terms for these ten
subject-predicate relations: 1) *cause*, p. 6; 2) *effect*, p. 20; 3) *subiect*, p. 22;

treatment of invention is devoted to the discussion and illustration of these subject-predicate relations and their species, which he conceives as so many seats or places where proof dwells.[20] As he deals with them in sequence, he refers constantly to Plato and Aristotle for support. Such works as Plato's *Timaeus, Phaedrus, Politicus, Parmenides,* and *Sophist* he cites more than once, while he quotes over and over again from Aristotle's writings, chiefly the *Topics, Rhetoric, Physics, Categories,* and *Metaphysics.*

In the second part of his dialectical system Ramus handles the subject of disposition, or judgment as he also calls it. Disposition is the process by which arguments, having been analyzed according to their subject-predicate relations, are put in shape for presentation. The patterns into which they are arranged take form as units of lesser or greater complexity, the least complicated being the proposition, the more complicated, the syllogism, and the most complicated, the logical discourse or treatise. Hence dialectical disposition has three aspects: the proposition, the syllogism, the method.[21] Ramus analyzes each of these aspects in turn, and thus gives the second part of dialectic a three-fold division.

What Ramus had to say on method was to exercise a considerable influence upon the writing of learned treatises during the sixteenth and seventeenth century. "Method," he explains, "is disposition by means of which the thing of premier importance among many things is put in the first place, the thing of secondary importance in the second place, the thing of tertiary importance in the third place, and so on."[22] He goes on to say that method is of two sorts. There is first the natural method, in which the writer, ded-

---

4) *adioinct,* p. 23; 5) *opposez,* p. 27; 6) *comparez,* p. 33; 7) *raison du nom,* p. 46; 8) *distribution,* p. 48; 9) *definition,* p. 58; 10) *authoritez* or *tesmoignages,* p. 61.

[20] *Dialectique,* 1555, p. 5.   [21] *Ibid.,* p. 71.

[22] *Ibid.,* p. 119. Translation mine. The French text reads: "Methode est disposition, par laquelle entre plusieurs choses la premiere de notice est disposée au premier lieu, la deuziesme au deuziesme, la troiziesme au troiziesme & ainsi consequemment."

icating himself to a severe economy and absolute discipline, uses the order of importance among things in nature as the order of importance among things in discourse.[23] Thus the general statement precedes the less general, the particular precedes the singular, and the singular precedes the example, which is the most specific of all the units of literary structure. The second type of method Ramus calls the prudential.[24] A writer follows it when he arranges his materials, not in the order of importance among things in nature, but in the order in which a reader would be most likely to receive them with least effort and greatest understanding.[25] This method is to be followed in any address to the populace, whom Ramus unflatteringly calls, "the beast of many heads,"[26] and "the vexatious and mulish auditor,"[27] whereas the natural method is to be followed in scientific writing.[28] In other words, the prudential method is that which accounts for the structure of orations and poems; the natural method, for the structure of scientific and learned treatises. It should be remarked in passing that Ramus' interest in the difference between the structure of the learned treatise and the structure of the popular address is a milestone in the transition from ancient rhetoric, with its emphasis upon argumentative forms, to modern rhetoric, with its added concern for exposition. It should also be remarked that the order in which Ramus' dialectical system is presented to the reader is a perfect illustration of the method he recommended for learned treatises. Nor were his followers unaware of this. Commenting upon the structure of the *Dialecticae Libri Duo*, MacIlmaine says:

The definition as most generall is first placed, next folowethe the diuision, first into the partes, and next into the formes and kyndes. Euery parte and forme is defined in his owne place, and made manifest by examples of auncient Authors, and last the members are limited and ioined togeather with short transitions for the recreation of the Reader.[29]

[23] *Ibid.*, p. 120.
[24] *Ibid.*, p. 120. Ramus' own words are: "Methode est de nature ou de prudence."
[25] *Ibid.*, p. 128.   [26] *Ibid.*, p. 129.   [27] *Ibid.*, p. 134.
[28] *Ibid.*, p. 128.   [29] *Op.cit.*, p. 12.

MacIlmaine adds that the natural method was observed by Plato, Aristotle, and all the ancient historiographers, orators, and poets, but later fell into disuse through ignorance, only to be rediscovered by Ramus. As I have mentioned, Ramus takes pains to stress the prudential as well as the natural method, and to associate the former with the types of discourse addressed to the populace. MacIlmaine tends, however, to see the natural method not only as the ancient pattern for oratory and poetry but also as the only pattern really recommended by Ramus. So in the course of time Ramus came to be regarded as the advocate of the natural method alone, and a great many treatises on the liberal arts written during the late sixteenth and early seventeenth century began abruptly with a definition, put next an enumeration of two major parts, followed this with a partition of each part into two minor parts, and so on, each of these movements being marked with brief transitions. It was this kind of organization which Bacon had in mind when in his own discussion of method in *De Dignitate et Augmentis Scientiarum* he spoke as follows of his predecessor Ramus:

And herein Ramus merited better in reviving those excellent rules of propositions (that they should be true, universally, primarily, and essentially), than he did in introducing his uniform method and dichotomies.[30]

In the last of the prefaces which he wrote for his *Dialecticae Libri Duo*, Ramus recalls that Archimedes had wished to have engraved on his tomb his discourse on the sphere and cylinder. "And as for me," says Ramus, "if you wish to inform yourself about my vigils and my studies, I shall wish the column of my sepulchre to be taken up with

[30] J. Spedding, R. L. Ellis, and D. D. Heath, *The Works of Francis Bacon*, 15 vols., Boston, 1860-1864, vol. 9, p. 128; vol. 2, p. 434. In the *Advancement of Learning*, the 1605 English version of what was published in 1623 as *De Dignitate et Augmentis Scientiarum*, Bacon criticizes Ramus for having introduced, not the "uniform method and dichotomies," but "the Canker of *Epitomes*." See *The Tvvoo Bookes of Francis Bacon. Of the proficience and aduancement of Learning, diuine and humane*, London, 1605, Bk. 2, p. 65ro.

my principles of the art of logic or dialectic."[31] Thus did he express his own hope that he would be remembered for his contribution to logic rather than for his other work. How far this hope was realized may be seen in the statement of his biographer and countryman that the *Dialectique*, published in 1555, is the most important philosophical work in French prior to Descartes' *Discours de la Méthode*.[32] As for the importance Ramus attached to logic as a subject of knowledge, quite apart from his own contribution to it, it need only be remarked that he believed God to be the perfect logician, that he believed man to be superior to the beasts because of his capacity to reason syllogistically, and that he believed one man superior to another only so far as he was superior in arranging his discourse according to the right method.[33]

Ramus' two principal works on rhetoric are the *Brutinae Quaestiones in Oratorem Ciceronis*, first published in 1547, and the *Rhetoricae Distinctiones in Quintilianum*, dated two years later. These two works apparently became the *Scholae Rhetoricae* in Ramus' *Scholae in Liberales Artes* (Basel, 1569). At any rate, the *Scholae Rhetoricae* consists of twenty books of criticism of Cicero and Quintilian, with Ramus interested in testing their rhetorical writings against his three laws.[34] The program which Ramus had in mind for rhetoric, as has already been partly indicated, was that it should abandon all its ancient topics except style and delivery, and in its treatment of style should deal only with tropes and figures. This program is indicated in general terms in the *Dialectique* and more particularly in the

---

[31] *La Dialectique de M. Pierre de la Ramee*, Paris, 1576, sig. a IIr°. Translation mine. This French version is not the same as that published in 1555. Ramus prepared the earlier one himself. The later one was done after Ramus' death as a new translation of the *Dialecticae Libri Duo*. See C. Waddington-Kastus, *De Petri Rami vita, scriptis, philosophia*, Paris, 1848, p. 177. For the allusion to Archimedes in Ramus' Latin words, see *P. Rami Dialecticae Libri Duo*, Paris, 1574, p. 2.

[32] Waddington, *Ramus*, p. 106.

[33] *Dialectique*, 1555, pp. 139, 118-19, 135-36.

[34] *Scholae Rhetoricae*, columns 238, 319-34, 339, 362, 364, 377, in *P. Rami Scholae in Liberales Artes*.

Scholae Rhetoricae.[35] But the execution of the program in a work that would parallel Ramus' *Dialecticae Libri Duo* was reserved for his colleague and friend, Audomarus Talaeus, also known as Omer Talon.

In 1544, one year after Ramus had launched his plans for reform of the liberal arts by publishing his *Dialecticae Institutiones* and *Aristotelicae Animadversiones*, which were as I have said the forerunners of the dialectical system just described, Audomarus Talaeus published at Paris his *Institutiones Oratoriae*. In later editions (the fifth appeared in 1552) this work came to be known as the *Rhetorica*. It was inserted in its entirety in Antoine Fouquelin's *La Rhétorique Françoise* (Paris, 1555, 1557).[36] It was published after Talaeus' death by Ramus, who added his own commentary to the text his friend had composed, even as Talaeus had edited and commented upon Ramus' *Dialecticae Libri Duo* a few years earlier.[37] Ramus' edition of the *Rhetorica* was printed several times during the latter part of the sixteenth century. In the preface to the first edition of the *Institutiones Oratoriae*, Talaeus had remarked that his work, despite its lack of finish, complemented what Ramus had been doing in the *Dialecticae Institutiones* and the *Aristotelicae Animadversiones*.[38] A preface to a later edition contains a more precise statement of what Talaeus felt to be the terms of the partnership between himself and Ramus in the reform of the liberal arts. He remarks that Ramus had been engaged in removing impurities from the doctrines of invention, disposition, and memory, and had returned these doctrines to dialectic, where they properly belong. Meanwhile, continues Talaeus, I myself with the assistance of Ramus' lectures and observations have called

[35] *Dialectique*, 1555, p. 134; *Scholae Rhetoricae*, columns 238, 290-93, in *Scholae in Liberales Artes*.

[36] "Talon, Omer," *Biographie Universelle, Ancienne et Moderne*.

[37] See Waddington, *Ramus*, pp. 464, 453, 443. According to Waddington, Talaeus edited Ramus' *Dialecticae Libri Duo* in 1556, this being its first Latin edition in two books. Waddington also indicates that Ramus first edited Talaeus' *Rhetorica* in 1567.

[38] *P. Rami & A. Talaei Collectaneae Praefationes, Epistolae, Orationes*, pp. 14-15.

rhetoric back to style and delivery, the only parts it can rightfully claim; and I have explained rhetoric by genus and species, illustrating it by examples from the orators and poets.[39] This avowal amounts to a confession that Talaeus is operating within the framework of Ramus' law of justice, which denies the possibility that rhetoric and dialectic can share the doctrine of invention and arrangement. As for what Talaeus actually did in carrying out his share of Ramus' program, it may be said that his *Rhetorica* is in the spirit not only of Ramus' law of justice but also of his other two laws. Talaeus begins by defining rhetoric as the art of speaking well, and by dividing it into style and delivery.[40] Each of these parts is then divided into two, style being given the subject of tropes and figures, while delivery is made to comprise voice and gesture.[41] The various species of tropes and figures are the concern of the first book. The second book is given over to the rules of articulation and action. The work as a whole is arranged so that there is a progress from the more general truths of rhetoric to the less general, until the particular example is reached; and this arrangement, of course, is in accord not only with Ramus' law of wisdom but also with his rules for the natural method. The definition with which the treatise begins, and the other more particular definitions, are all in the spirit of Ramus' law of truth—the predicates are formed, that is, so that they are valid for every case belonging under their subject, at least in a formal sense. In fact, Talaeus' *Rhetorica* is so close in spirit to Ramus' *Dialecticae Libri Duo*, and Ramus so far overshadowed his colleague in fame, that we can understand why there have been attempts to deny the existence of Talaeus, and to allege that Ramus invented the name in order to shield himself against the envy of his enemies and to put himself in a position where he could praise his own works under the pretense of praising those

[39] *Ibid.*, pp. 15-16.
[40] *Audomari Talaei Rhetorica e P. Rami Praelectionibus observata*, Per Claudium Minoem, Frankfurt, 1582, pp. 25-26.
[41] *Ibid.*, pp. 30, 168.

of a friend.[42] There was even one editor of Talaeus' *Rhetorica* who published it under the name of Ramus. He was Charles Butler, an Englishman, who, in bringing out the *Rhetorica* at Oxford in 1597, called it *Rameae Rhetoricae Libri Duo*. Three years later, however, Butler again issued this work at the same place, with 42 chapters instead of the 47 of his first edition. This time he omitted Ramus' name from the title without substituting that of Talaeus. Incidentally, it was this edition of the *Rhetoricae Libri Duo*, and its derivatives, which carried Talaeus' *Rhetorica* into the minds of English schoolboys during the entire course of the seventeenth century.[43]

When he discusses tropes and figures as the stylistic movement of rhetoric, Talaeus not only draws upon such influential and standard authorities as the 8th and 9th books of Quintilian's *Institutio Oratoria*, but also, by virtue of his insistence that tropes and figures are the only constituents of style, he says in effect that the successful pattern of language in oratorical effort is any exceptional, unusual, or extraordinary pattern. Tropes, it will be remembered, are taken by him and indeed by all his contemporaries to mean words employed outside of their normal contexts, as when metonymies, ironies, metaphors, and synecdoches are used. Figures, also called schemes from the term given them in Greek, represent in the aggregate to Talaeus and his contemporaries all the possible ways of arranging unusual, uncustomary language patterns, as when words are clustered into rhythms, meters, periodic measures, repetitions, climaxes, and the like. Thus tropes and figures both indicate the state of affairs when language is doing something it does not ordinarily do. And Talaeus, by making these doings the sole criteria of effectiveness in speech, endorses the view that good style is a flight from the natural, and

[42] For an examination of these allegations, see Waddington, *Ramus*, pp. 475, 464.

[43] See [John Brinsley,] *Ludus Literarius: or, The Grammar Schoole*, London, 1612, pp. 203-4. See also Charles Hoole, *A New Discovery Of the old Art of Teaching Schoole*, Ed. by E. T. Campagnac, Liverpool, 1913 [part III], pp. 132-33. Hoole wrote in 1659.

that anybody who words a thing as people would word it on everyday occasions is being ineffective. True effectiveness, he plainly implies, consists in the systematic repudiation of the normal patterns of communication. Unlike Quintilian, whose discussion of style is not confined to tropes and figures, and whose implication is that only the elevated subject produces the sublime utterance, with unusual ornaments as its necessary features, Talaeus seems to be saying throughout his first book that the elevated, unusual style and the profusion of ornaments are the only choices ever open to the orator who would be truly effective.

Talaeus' rules for voice and gesture produce a different sort of unnaturalness from that just discussed. He does not recommend that voice and action in oratory should stand opposed to voice and action in normal situations. But he does not found his discussion of delivery upon the principle that the normal pattern and the oratorical pattern are both responses to the speaker's sense of meaning. He implies instead that these patterns are responses to the speaker's sense of the appropriate rule. Thus in effect he tells the orator that the response will be right if the rule is followed, not that the response will be right if conditions exist so as to make that response truly reflect the speaker's pattern of thought and feeling. A few of these rules, as translated by Abraham Fraunce in the *Arcadian Rhetorike*, will give an idea of all the others. Says Fraunce of voice:

In pitie and lamentation, the voyce must be full, sobbing, flexible, interrupted. . . . In anger, shrill, sharpe, quicke, short. . . . In feare and bashfulnesse, contracted, stammering, trembling. . . . In ioy, gladnes, or pleasure, tender, mild, sweetlie flowing. . . . In anguish and griefe of mind without compassion, a hollow voyce fetcht from the bottome of the throate, groaning.[44]

[44] *The Arcadian Rhetorike*, London, [1588], sig. i2 vo-i5 ro. For these rules in Talaeus, see *A. Talaei Rhetorica e P. Rami Praelectionibus Observata,* Per C. Minoem, pp. 178. 25-26; 179. 1-3; 179. 15-16; 179. 26-27; 180. 3-4. *The Arcadian Rhetorike* is second in time among the English translations of Talaeus' *Rhetorica*. The first is by Dudley Fenner, who in 1584 brought out at Middelburg Ramus' *Dialecticae Libri Duo* and Talaeus' *Rhetorica* under

Ramus' system of dialectic and Talaeus' system of rhetoric did not mean that the power to grasp and order proof should have no place in the orator's equipment, or that the power to speak in ornaments and rule-made accents was something you acquired by itself without reference to your analytical and conceptual ability. As Ramus and Talaeus presented their theory of communication to their own students, they emphasized the close union of philosophy and eloquence, or of logical and verbal skill.[45] They did not seek to divorce logical factors from presentational factors in the process of communication. They sought, rather, to group the logical factors under one heading, called dialectic, and the presentational factors under another heading, called rhetoric, and to divorce them merely for convenience in teaching. Thus, while the student was concentrating upon the logical aspects of discourse, he was not forced to pay any heed at that moment to the stylistic aspects; he would get that training almost immediately afterwards in his class in rhetoric, where no stress was placed upon logic. But although Ramus and Talaeus cannot be accused of sponsoring the idea of an ornamental rhetoric that has no logical force, or of a philosophical presentation that has no concern with stylistic effectiveness, the fact is that their particular way of separating rhetoric and dialectic was not entirely fortunate. What they did was to assume that the process of communication was a whole which could be divided into parts at the point where analysis and synthesis ceased to operate and where the problems of style and delivery began to demand attention. Had they been thoroughly Aristotelian, they would have assumed, as I mentioned earlier, that the process of communication was made

---

the title, *The Artes of Logike and Rethorike.* Fenner does not, however, translate that part of Talaeus which concerns delivery. Fraunce also translated Ramus' *Dialecticae Libri Duo* as the basis of his *Lawiers Logike*, London, 1588.

[45] Talaeus states this as the principal tenet of the reforms he and Ramus were seeking. See *P. Rami & A. Talaei Collectaneae Praefationes, Epistolae, Orationes*, p. 14. For their methods of collaboration as teachers, see Waddington, *Ramus*, pp. 33, 64-65; also Graves, *Peter Ramus*, pp. 28-29, 38-40.

up of two wholes, one of which involved analysis and synthesis of speculative questions before a learned audience,
and the other of which involved these same two intellectual
powers, and in addition the command of style and delivery,
before the popular audience and upon the question of legal
or political policy. In other words, Aristotle, and his disciple Cicero, thought of dialectic and rhetoric as two distinct arts which shared similar intellectual procedures and
sought to discharge respectively the related but by no means
identical offices of conviction and persuasion. Ramus and
Talaeus thought of dialectic and rhetoric as two distinct
arts which divided between them on a purely mathematical
basis the four intellectual procedures of composition, and
sought to discharge respectively the related but by no means
identical offices of conviction and verbal stimulation. It
would not be too much to say that Ramus and Talaeus held
to the ancient notion of dialectic as the theory of conviction,
while abolishing the ancient notion of rhetoric as the theory of persuasion and substituting for it the notion of rhetoric as the theory of verbal ingenuity and ornament. This
latter notion, which could not in itself create an ornamental oratory at the expense of a persuasive oratory, did in fact
find congenial surroundings in western Europe of the sixteenth and early seventeenth century, where persuasive oratory was not a vital part of political and religious life. The
fact that political power was vested at that time in a heredi-
tary monarch and aristocracy, who were not required to win
the consent of the masses by constant appeals to reason,
made it inevitable that the effective pattern of language in
oratory would be defined in terms of its power to compliment and flatter the master rather than to conciliate the
servant. Talaeus' rhetorical doctrine, with its emphasis
upon the necessity of saying things in uncustomary ways,
more easily served the commoner in his quest for political
favors from the aristocrat than it served the aristocrat,
whose political and social position did not depend upon his
currying favors with the commoners. Moreover, the church
at that time felt its original task of conversion to have been

largely accomplished at home, and felt also that conversion itself was rather the great miracle of Christianity than the direct result of the reasonings and persuasions of men. These notions encouraged the assumption that pulpit eloquence need be merely ceremonial and ornamental. This assumption, in turn, made the rhetoric of Talaeus seem entirely adequate as a means of preparing young men for the ministry. Thus cultural pressures were acting to force oratory to become ceremonial at the time when Talaeus' rhetoric of ornament was being introduced into education as part of the reforms of Ramus. Those pressures were well suited to that rhetoric, as it was well suited to them. They complemented each other in depriving oratory of the significance it has when men use it as an instrument of leadership. Oratory became ingenious and empty. Speaking in 1605 of the intellectual awakening of the preceding century, Francis Bacon mentions that the men of that time eagerly studied to be eloquent. He then says:

This grew speedily to an excesse: for men began to hunt more after wordes, than matter, and more after the choisenesse of the Phrase, and the round and cleane composition of the sentence, and the sweet falling of the clauses, and the varying and illustration of their workes with tropes and figures: then after the weight of matter, worth of subiect, soundnesse of argument, life of inuention, or depth of iudgement.[46]

"In summe," he adds, after naming those who had sought the eloquence just described, and including Ramus' teacher Sturm among them, "the whole inclination and bent of those times, was rather towards copie, than weight."[47] Then he concludes with words which perfectly diagnose the cultural maladies behind such a movement as that which Talaeus' rhetoric implemented:

Here therefore, the first distemper of learning, when men studie words, and not matter: whereof though I haue represented an example of late times: yet it hath beene, and will be *Secundum*

[46] *The Tvvoo Bookes of Francis Bacon. Of the proficience and aduancement of Learning*, London, 1605, Bk. 1, pp. 18ro-18vo.
[47] *Ibid.*, Bk. 1, p. 18vo.

24

maius & minus in all time. . . . It seemes to me that *Pigmalions* frenzie is a good embleme or portraiture of this vanitie: for wordes are but the Images of matter, and except they haue life of reason and inuention: to fall in loue with them, is all one, as to fall in loue with a Picture.[48]

Bacon's dissatisfaction was directed, not specifically at the rhetorical doctrine of Talaeus, but rather at the large tendencies which had made that doctrine popular during the sixteenth century. Even as Bacon published *The Advancement of Learning,* those tendencies were losing momentum, and new social pressures were preparing the way for reforms in the learned arts. One pressure developed as men realized that, while the religious community of western Europe did not face at home the problem of converting heathens to Christianity, it did nevertheless face in the spread of Protestantism a movement which required more than brute force to arrest it, more than silent faith to promote it. Serious Catholics and Protestants alike came to see that the sermon should be regarded less as an opportunity to display verbal skill than as a positive instrument in furthering their respective causes. Another pressure, created perhaps by the writings of Bacon and Descartes, was felt more and more as men discovered new scientific truths through the process of experimentation, and found that a theory of communication based upon the tropes and figures and upon Ramus' conception of expository method did not serve the needs of the scientist. When these pressures became acute towards the middle of the seventeenth century, the learned world began to revise the theory of logic and rhetoric, and it is as one such revision that Fénelon's *Dialogues on Eloquence* are to be regarded.

Before we turn to Fénelon, we should observe that, when he was only eleven years old, there occurred in the field of logic a reform which, less by virtue of its originality than of its popular appeal, may be said to have ended the influence of Ramus' dialectical system. This reform was the work of Antoine Arnauld. In 1662 Arnauld brought out at

48 *Ibid.,* Bk. 1 pp. 18vo-19ro.

Paris his celebrated *Logique ou L'Art de Penser*. It became a phenomenal success, almost monopolizing its field for two centuries after its publication. One of its later editors remarked that it cast into oblivion all similar works produced up to its time, without having been cast into oblivion itself by any similar works produced thereafter.[49] Before he published the *Logique*, Arnauld was well known as an advocate of Jansenism and as an associate of a like-minded group of theologians and teachers who lodged at Port-Royal near Paris and conducted the celebrated "little schools" of Port-Royal. One of the leading teachers at Port-Royal, Pierre Nicole, is in part responsible for the *Logique*, and is usually named as its joint author,[50] but for convenience I shall speak of it as if it belonged wholly to Arnauld. In the course of time, the *Logique* came to be known in France as the *Logique de Port-Royal* and in England as *The Port Royal Logic*. Arnauld himself acknowledges that *The Port Royal Logic* depends for its traditional materials upon Aristotle's treatises, and for its new materials upon Pascal's *De l'Esprit Géométrique*, and upon various writings of Descartes, notably the *Discours de la Méthode*.[51] Arnauld also makes specific reference to Gassendi's *Institutio Logica*[52] and borrows from it the notion that logic has four parts. It should moreover be remarked that *The Port Royal Logic* mentions Hobbes, Montaigne, Fludd, and many others, notably Saint Augustine.[53] But it is unwary to assume, as Sainte-Beuve and Waddington do, that Arnauld also depends for guidance and doctrine upon Ramus' *Dialectique* of 1555.[54] What Arnauld does instead is to attack the valid

[49] [G. Du Pac de Bellegarde and J. Hautefage,] *Œuvres de Messire Antoine Arnauld*, 42 vols., Paris, 1775-1781, vol. 41, p. iv.

[50] *Ibid.*, pp. iv, 103, 104.

[51] *Ibid.*, pp. 110, 122, 332, 367-68. Arnauld's rules for convincing the mind (pp. 368-70) are taken from Pascal's *De l'Art de Persuader*, which Arnauld considered to be part of the *Esprit Géométrique*.

[52] *Ibid.*, p. 131; for other references to Gassendi, see pp. 318-21.

[53] *Ibid.*, pp. 130, 333-35, 121, 161, etc. Arnauld's references to Saint Augustine are very numerous, and I shall make no attempt to list any of them here.

[54] C.-A. Sainte-Beuve, *Port-Royal*, Ed. by R.-L. Doyon and C. Marchesné, 10 vols., Paris, 1926-1932, vol. 5, pp. 73, 77; Waddington, *Ramus*, p. 377.

ity of Ramus' system and to seek in a spirit of respect and firmness to rid the learned world of its sense of obligation to that still-potent master.

"Ramus and his adherents," observes Arnauld as he speaks in *The Port Royal Logic* of the process of dividing wholes into parts, "torment themselves greatly to show that all divisions ought to have only two members."[55] These words refer, of course, to Ramus' habit of dividing each of the liberal disciplines into two and only two parts, as when he insists that grammar is to be split into etymology and syntax, rhetoric into style and delivery, dialectic into invention and judgment.[56] It is noteworthy that Arnauld does not adopt this formula as the organizing principle of *The Port Royal Logic*. Instead, as I have already indicated, he divides logic into four parts, not two, and he names these parts as Gassendi, not as Ramus, had done. Thus he speaks of logic as the system of reflections men have made upon the four chief operations of the human mind: conceiving, judging, reasoning, ordering.[57] To each of these operations he assigns a main division of his work. His first division analyzes not only the concept, as a mental phenomenon, but also its linguistic equivalent, the term. The modern student of semantics would find much to interest him in this part of *The Port Royal Logic*. Arnauld's second division deals with the act of judgment as that act expresses itself in the logical proposition. His third part covers syllogisms and fallacies, the latter subject being treated with freshness and brilliance. In his final division, he has in mind discourse itself as the largest of the phenomena studied by logic, and what he says on this subject he entitles "De la Méthode."[58] Although he discusses two sorts of method, there is a marked difference otherwise between his approach and that of Ramus. As we have seen, the latter

[55] *Œuvres de Arnauld*, vol. 41, p. 243. Translation mine.
[56] See above, pp. 11, 16. See also Ramus' *Dialectique* (1555), pp. 123, 134, 4.
[57] *Œuvres de Arnauld*, vol. 41, p. 125. Compare with P. Gassendi, *Opera Omnia*, 6 vols., Lyons, 1658, vol. 1, pp. 33-34, 91.
[58] *Œuvres de Arnauld*, vol. 41, p. 354.

had proposed the natural and the prudential method, both of which had to do with presentation, the one to the learned, the other to the popular, audience. Arnauld proposes the method of analysis, which is used by the thinker in proceeding from the known to the unknown in the discovery of truth, and the method of synthesis, which is used by writer or speaker, and which consists in passing from the general and simple to the specific and complex.[59] The method of synthesis, as Arnauld presents it, takes its principles from Pascal's *De L'Art de Persuader*; the method of analysis, from the four steps prescribed in Descartes' *Discours de la Méthode*. There is yet another difference between Ramus' attitude towards method and that of Arnauld. By his own procedure as writer and by his theory of discourse as well, Ramus had indicated that one subdivision of a discourse should not contain anything belonging to another subdivision. Arnauld thinks otherwise. In fact, he seems to have Ramus' very rule in mind when he makes the following statement:

It is also well to give notice that the author [Arnauld] has excused himself from following all the while the rules of a method altogether exact, and has put in the fourth part many things which he would have been able to refer to the second and to the third.[60]

Nowhere in *The Port Royal Logic* is the spirit of protest against Ramus more in evidence than it is where Arnauld discusses the doctrine of the places. It will be recalled that Ramus reduced this doctrine to ten subject-predicate relations and made the discussion of it the mathematical half of the science of dialectic. Arnauld includes it under protest, not as something useful and important, but as something short, easy, familiar, and formerly celebrated by famous writers.[61] In the chapter he devotes to showing how useless these places are, Arnauld first mentions their position as that part of logic which is called invention and their priority over the other part of logic in the system of Ra-

[59] *Ibid.*, pp. 362, 366-70.   [60] *Ibid.*, p. 114. Translation mine.
[61] *Ibid.*, pp. 111, 304-5.

28

mus.[62] He pauses here to express the opinion that Ramus' argument for giving invention the first place in logic, and disposition the second, is downright feeble.[63] Next he proceeds to make the whole doctrine of places the object of a withering attack. Recalling the importance of this doctrine in the dialectical and rhetorical writings of Aristotle, Cicero, and Quintilian, Arnauld proposes that one would have no choice but to share the views of these august authorities if experience itself did not appear to be entirely opposed to this part of their teaching. Then he says:

In this connection you can take as your witnesses almost as many persons as there are among those who have passed through the regular course of study and have learned to seek proofs by this artificial method as it is taught in the schools. For is there a single one of them who can truly say that, when he has been obliged to handle some subject or other, he based his reflections upon these places, and searched in them for the arguments which he needed? Consult as many barristers, as many preachers, as there are in the world, and as many men who speak and write and who always have subject matter enough and to spare, and I do not know if you will be able to find a single one of them who could always intentionally make an argument *à causa, ab effectu, ab adjunctis*, in order to prove that which he wished to prove.[64]

Thus does Arnauld demolish what Ramus had made the half of logic. But he does not rest his case at this point. He goes on to say that arguments are to be found on any subject, not by referring to the "heads" and "general terms" which are called places, but by referring to nature, by considering the particular subject closely, and by knowing diverse truths.[65] Then he indulges in some mild ridicule of Ramus' suggestion that a knowledge of the places of logic prompts poetic invention. He quotes a speech from the ninth book of Virgil's *Aeneid* and then comments as follows:

Ramus declares that this is an argument *à causa efficiente;* but one would be able to take a rather confident oath that Virgil

62 *Ibid.*, p. 301.
63 *Ibid.*, pp. 301-2.
64 *Ibid.*, p. 302. Translation mine.
65 *Ibid.*, p. 303.

never dreamed of the place of efficient cause when he made these verses. He would never have made them if he had paused to search for this thought in that place.[66]

Despite the warmth of Arnauld's opposition to the doctrine of places in Ramus' logic, it must be remembered, as I mentioned earlier, that he devotes a chapter to that subject. But there are two things to be observed in his treatment of it. First, his chapter is brief and perfunctory. Secondly, he says that he will not follow Cicero and Quintilian, on the ground that they treat the places with too little method; nor Ramus, on the ground that he loaded them down with too many subdivisions. Instead he decides to take the German philosopher Clauberg as his authority.[67]

Not only does *The Port Royal Logic* break with Ramus on the whole question of method in discourse and on the question of the value of places; it also breaks with Ramus on the propriety of the departmentalization of the liberal disciplines. Under the law of justice, as I have said, Ramus holds that one art should contain nothing whatever that belongs to another—that logic must say nothing proper to rhetoric, rhetoric nothing proper to logic. That this law was still influential in Arnauld's day is indicated by one of the criticisms made against the first edition of *The Port Royal Logic*. These criticisms Arnauld himself enumerates in a special discourse prefixed to the second and all later editions. It appears in this discourse that the *Logic* had been unfavorably regarded for dealing, not exclusively with logic, but with a medley of logic, rhetoric, ethics, metaphysics, and geometry.[68] Arnauld's retort is in part facetious. He says that a book cannot have a greater fault than that of not being read, and that a mixture of many things attracts more readers than does a thing treated dryly and methodically by itself.[69] But his real reason for the medley, he goes on, is that logic is not an isolated study, but the instrument of all other sciences, and it should never be presented as if it were devoid of immediate connection with

[66] *Ibid.*, p. 304. Translation mine. [67] *Ibid.*, p. 305.
[68] *Ibid.*, p. 116. [69] *Ibid.*, p. 117.

them.[70] At this point he states a thesis quite contrary to that which led Ramus to separate logic and rhetoric with such utter completeness. Rhetoric, argues Arnauld, claims to do several things, but its true job is to prevent certain bad ways of writing and speaking, above all that worst of all vices, an artificial and rhetorical style laden with false and exaggerated thoughts and forced figures.[71] There is in my logic, Arnauld continues, as much that can be used to avoid these faults as one would find in the ordinary rhetoric. In proof of this, he points to his later analysis of the plain and figured style as giving the rule for determining whether a figure is good or bad, his treatment of the places as showing how to avoid the empty superfluity of the obvious, his discussion of sophisms as teaching how never to accept the false for the beautiful. This latter doctrine, he says, is one of the most important rules of the true rhetoric and more than any other can form the mind to a simple, natural, and judicious style.[72] Another principle of the true rhetoric, says Arnauld, is found in Pascal's notion that references to self on the speaker's part tend to stir up the latent envy, malice, and jealousy of the hearer.[73] Doctrines such as these Arnauld considers to be the property of rhetoric. But he includes them in his logic because he thinks they also belong there. In other words, he does not seem impressed by the argument that the proper procedure is for each liberal discipline to emphasize the ways in which it differs from the others, and to deny the possibility that there are areas which these disciplines may fruitfully share in common. That he had Ramus in mind when he deliberately included rhetorical doctrine within his logic is proved by his own words. He says:

Everything which owes obedience to logic belongs to it. And entirely ridiculous are such things as the tortures certain authors give themselves, like Ramus and the Ramists, though

[70] *Ibid.*, pp. 117-18.   [71] *Ibid.*, p. 118.
[72] *Ibid.*, p. 118. The rule that there is nothing beautiful but what is true is explained more fully by Arnauld on p. 343.
[73] *Ibid.*, pp. 118, 331-35.

31

otherwise very learned folk, who take as many pains to limit the jurisdictions of each science, and to see that one does not impinge upon another, as one takes to mark the frontiers of kingdoms and to regulate the powers of parliaments.[74]

There are three other indications in *The Port Royal Logic*, in addition to those already enumerated, of Arnauld's interest in freeing the learned world of the heavy weight of Ramus' theory of communication. When he says, for example, that he deliberately chose to give his work the subtitle, *The Art of Thinking*, rather than the more usual one, *The Art of Thinking Well*, his preference not only reminds us that it was Ramus' favorite practice to put the word "well" in the definition of each liberal art, but also suggests that, so far as Arnauld is concerned, the practice has outlived its usefulness.[75] Secondly, when Arnauld says that he regards the traditional rules of the syllogism as less useful than they are usually taken to be,[76] and when he reminds his readers a few pages later that the nine chapters devoted to these rules are of scant use,[77] we can take his statements to be as comprehensive an attack on Ramus' logic as was the condemnation of the places. Thirdly, when Arnauld takes the position that the principles of logic are designed primarily as aids in the understanding of things and in the instruction of others in that understanding,[78] he repudiates the idea of Ramus that the principles of logic are designed as aids in the conduct of disputes. Disputing, Arnauld says later, is not to be condemned in general, and when good use is made of it, "there is nothing that better serves to provide diverse openings either to finding out truth or to instilling it in others."[79] Even so, *The Port Royal Logic* is not a treatise on dispute as the cardinal activity in the pursuit of truth. It is rather a direct inquiry into the

[74] *Ibid.*, p. 113. Translation mine.
[75] *Dialectique* (1555), pp. IIv⁰, 2, 58; also *Œuvres de Arnauld*, vol. 41, p. 116.
[76] *Œuvres de Arnauld*, vol. 41, p. 254.
[77] *Ibid.*, p. 258, note.   [78] *Ibid.*, p. 125.
[79] *Ibid.*, p. 335. Translation mine.

pursuit of truth, and into the rules which govern the mind in seeking and stating the knowledge of things.

Arnauld's campaign to destroy the influence of Ramus' logic had one important effect before Fénelon composed his *Dialogues on Eloquence*. That effect can be seen in a famous French treatise on the art of speaking published anonymously at Paris in 1675 under the title, *De L'Art de Parler*. Thirteen years later, in its third edition, this treatise was called *La Rhétorique, ou L'Art de Parler*, and Bernard Lamy was acknowledged as its author. Meanwhile, it had been published at London in an English translation, which had attributed it to the "Messieurs du Port Royal,"[80] and thus it is sometimes called *The Port Royal Rhetoric*. Actually Lamy had no connection with the Port-Royal group. He was instead a member of the Congregation of the Oratory, a society of priests who conducted schools and sponsored educational reforms similar to those of the Port-Royalists.[81] But his *De L'Art de Parler* does have a connection with Arnauld's reform of logic. That connection might well be described by saying that Lamy is bent upon compromise —that he shows positive traces of loyalty to Ramus and Talaeus, on the one hand, and to Arnauld, on the other. Thus he achieves, not a true Port-Royal rhetoric, and not a true Ramist rhetoric, but a mixture of the two.

Lamy's loyalty to Ramus and Talaeus is not shown in any open manner. He does not mention these two authorities in the entire text of *De L'Art de Parler*. But there are at least two things in his work which can be explained only in terms of his sense of obligation to what Ramus had stood for. The first of these things is his refusal to treat "the art of speaking" and "the art of persuasion"

---

[80] The title-page of the first edition of the English translation reads: *The Art of Speaking*: Written in French by Messieurs du Port Royal: In pursuance of a former Treatise, Intituled, *The Art of Thinking*. Rendred into English. London, Printed by W. Godbid, and are to be Sold by M. Pitt, at the *Angel* against the little North Door of St. *Paul's* Church. 1676.

[81] The schools of the Oratorians and those of Port-Royal are compared by H. C. Barnard, *The Little Schools of Port-Royal*, Cambridge, 1913, pp. 205-7.

as one and the same art. He admits that the ancients had treated them together. But he confesses himself unable to follow their example. The difference between the two arts, he says, is that he who possesses the art of speaking does not necessarily know the secret of gaining the heart and mind of an audience. "This," he continues, "is why, being obliged to treat of these two arts, I believed I ought to do it separately."[82] His belief that he ought to keep the two arts distinct is an acknowledgment of his adherence to Ramus' law of justice. As we know, that law required rhetoric to avoid any subject claimed more properly by dialectic. For example, rhetoric could not deal with persuasion, since dialectic already treated the subject of conviction, the largest (and certainly the most respectable) part of the process of influencing conduct. In rejecting persuasion as the property of rhetoric, Lamy seems to consider rhetoric to be somehow an inviolate entity, incapable of attaching unto itself any subject deemed relevant by himself, or any subject deemed relevant by writers more ancient than Ramus. The second thing which shows Lamy's sense of obligation to Ramus is that he makes "the art of speaking" consist of materials drawn largely from the doctrine of style and delivery. Of the first four sections of *De L'Art de Parler*, Part II is devoted to the tropes and figures, Part III to pronunciation, periodic structure, and versification, and Part IV to the kinds of styles and rhetorical embellishments. It must be admitted that Lamy does not treat these subjects by a rigid method of definition, division, and subdivision, as Ramus and Talaeus did. It must also be admitted that Part I of *De L'Art de Parler* contains grammatical materials, which under Ramus' law of justice should not appear in a work on rhetoric. But in the two respects which I have just discussed, Lamy shows a marked tendency to operate within the context of Ramus' characteristic ideas.

Lamy also shows a marked tendency to operate within the

[82] *De L'Art de Parler*, Paris, 1676, p. 276. Translation mine. Lamy's words are as follows: "C'est pourquoy estant obligé de traitter de ces deux Arts, j'ay crû que je le devois faire separément."

context of Arnauld's thinking. Not only does he quote *The Port Royal Grammar*, which Arnauld wrote in collaboration with Claude Lancelot, but he also emphasizes the basic operations of the human mind in the very terms Arnauld used to name the four parts of logic.[83] Lamy is said to have greatly admired *The Port Royal Logic* and to have compiled an abridgement of it.[84] There can be no doubt that he knew it intimately, and that its eloquence incited him to undertake the task of reforming rhetoric. One evidence of Arnauld's influence can be seen in the fact that Lamy felt it necessary to attach an essay on persuasion to his "art of speaking." As we have noticed, *The Port Royal Logic* has several things to say about persuasion, and Arnauld defends his right to make statements about this subject in a work on logic. Lamy apparently decided that, if Arnauld found persuasion to be a topic of logic, then it would be at least admissible as a kind of appendix to a work on rhetoric. Another evidence of Arnauld's influence can be seen in the fact that Lamy in discussing persuasion lays emphasis upon the speaker's obligation not to speak of himself lest he alienate his audience,[85] a principle which Arnauld had stressed and had attributed to Pascal. Still another evidence of Arnauld's influence, and perhaps the plainest of all, is that Lamy accepts as material for his treatise on persuasion a generous amount of the ancient theory of invention and disposition, but when he comes to treat the doctrine of the places of logic and rhetoric, he admits it with great reluctance, emphasizing beforehand that serious meditation and long study are the only means of filling the mind with sure knowledge, and taking notice afterwards of the objections often raised against the use of places.[86] Here he models himself upon Arnauld in almost

[83] *Ibid.*, pp. 15, 16, 24. [84] Barnard, *op. cit.*, p. 207, note.
[85] *De L'Art de Parler*, p. 298.

[86] *Ibid.*, pp. 280-88, 289-91. In his study of Lamy's *De L'Art de Parler*, Douglas Ehninger thinks it a curious fact that Lamy should devote half of his discussion of invention to the doctrine of places, and then add a chapter condemning that doctrine. See his "Bernard Lami's *L'Art de Parler*: A Critical Analysis," *The Quarterly Journal of Speech*, 32 (1946) p.

every possible way. Still other evidences of his debt to Arnauld are seen here and there in his treatise in small but interesting ways: he borrows Arnauld's notion that words are signs of the ideas to which they are tied;[87] he uses for a simpler purpose the Virgilian passage which to Ramus meant poetic invention from the efficient cause, and to Arnauld meant invention without benefit of the places of logic;[88] he adopts and emphasizes Arnauld's aesthetic doctrine that there can be nothing beautiful which is not true.[89] Thus he achieves a rhetoric which, while bound to some of the pet ideas of the Ramists, and while unable to transcend Arnauld's reforms, is nevertheless fresh and forward-looking in spirit. Such words as these remain in one's mind after he has read *De L'Art de Parler*:

For in short, words being nothing but sound, we ought not to prefer their harmony to the solid knowledg of truth. For my own part I value not the Art of Speaking, but as it contributes to the discovery of truth; as it forces it from the bottom of our thoughts where it lay conceal'd; as it disintangles it, and displays it to our eyes; and indeed this is the true cause that has incouraged me to write of this Art, as a thing not only useful, but necessary.[90]

Let us now turn to Fénelon's *Dialogues on Eloquence*. This work, as I mentioned earlier, is a product of Fénelon's youth, and the best opinion would seem to be that Fénelon composed it about the year 1679,[91] seventeen years after the

---

434. Actually, however, Lamy's procedure at this point is not an unprecedented oddity unless we forget that he found authority for it in *The Port Royal Logic*.

[87] *De L'Art de Parler*, p. 41; *Œuvres de Arnauld*, vol. 41, p. 126.

[88] *De L'Art de Parler*, pp. 79-80; *Œuvres de Arnauld*, vol. 41, pp. 303-4. See above, p. 29.

[89] *De L'Art de Parler*, p. 263; *Œuvres de Arnauld*, vol. 41, pp. 118, 343.

[90] *De L'Art de Parler*, p. 266. Translation quoted from *The Art of Speaking*, by Messieurs du Port Royal, London, 1676, Part IV, pp. 76-77.

[91] For a survey of the evidence for believing that the *Dialogues* were composed in the year 1679, see C. Revillout, "Un problème de chronologie littéraire et philologique: date présumable des 'dialogues' de Fénelon 'sur l'éloquence,'" *Revue des Langues Romanes*, 33 (1889) pp. 5-30, 194-216. See also L. F. Bausset, *Histoire de Fénelon*, 3rd ed., 4 vols., Versailles, 1817, vol. 3, pp. 109, 120; also E. Carcassonne, *État présent des travaux sur Fénelon*, Paris, 1939, p. 109.

publication of the first edition of *The Port Royal Logic*, and four years after Lamy first published *De L'Art de Parler*. Although the *Dialogues* remained in manuscript until 1717, two years after Fénelon's death, and thus did not exert any influence upon opinion in the seventeenth century, they are nevertheless a product of that century, and a continuation of the reforms of Arnauld and Lamy in the field of rhetorical theory. Had the *Dialogues* been published at the time when they were written, they might have been entitled *The Port Royal Rhetoric* with better reason than was shown by those who associated *De L'Art de Parler* with the Port-Royalists. To be sure, Fénelon had no connection with that group of theologians and reformers. In fact, during his very early youth, the schools of Port-Royal had been finally dispersed under the pressure of the Jesuits and the anti-Jansenists. Moreover, although the great popularity of *The Port Royal Logic* during Fénelon's youth, and the importance of logic in the educational system of the time, would argue almost irresistibly that he knew Arnauld's book intimately, there is no evidence so far as I know to prove that he read it. Nevertheless, the *Dialogues* make common cause with *The Port Royal Logic* not only in sponsoring the same kind of new rhetoric but also in seeking to destroy the influence of the chief doctrines of Ramus and Talaeus.

It has already been emphasized that Ramus and Talaeus, in confining the theory of rhetorical style to the tropes and figures, had in fact defined effective expression as unusual expression, and had made the quest for good style a quest for every linguistic mode that offers any contrast to ordinary patterns of speech. It is to this theory of style that Fénelon strenuously objects in the *Dialogues*. He seeks everywhere to deny that the critic's interest in discourse is focused upon the question of unusual word order and the metaphorical dimensions of language. Early in the *Dialogues* he has his chief spokesman express this denial in terms of a comparison between Demosthenes and Isocrates:

The latter is a lifeless speaker who meant only to polish his thoughts and to give melody to his utterances. He had but a

37

low conception of eloquence, and he reduced it almost entirely to the arrangement of words. A man who according to some took ten years, and according to others, fifteen, to arrange the periods of his Panegyric, which is a speech on the needs of Greece, was of feeble and belated assistance to the republic against the enterprises of the king of Persia. Demosthenes spoke quite otherwise against Philip. . . . You only see in Isocrates a flowery and effeminate discourse, and periods contrived with infinite labor to please the ear, while Demosthenes moves, warms, and captivates the heart.[92]

This same protest against ornamental discourse is a recurrent theme of the *Dialogues*. Never is the reader permitted to forget that planted flowers, epigrams, riddles, conceits, verbal flourishes, word-play, antitheses, pomposity, puns, "elegant" phrases, purple patches, are not only the fashion of the pulpit in Fénelon's day, but also the ingredients of a low conception of eloquence.

As for the style which the true rhetoric should teach, Fénelon advocates a return to the way men actually communicate when their knowledge is deep and their sense of the needs of their fellow men is keen. This is the natural style. This is the simple and familiar style. This is the style in which tropes and figures appear, not because they have been learned from a book, but because the speaker, unconscious perhaps of their very names, finds them to be part of the language of strong conviction and powerful feeling. But it is the conviction and feeling which produce them; they are not to be cultivated for themselves. Fénelon never names or analyzes the tropes and figures which Talaeus had made the larger part of rhetoric. Thus he protests against that rhetoric by ignoring its contents and by keeping the reader's attention fixed upon the unhappy results it had produced wherever it had been tried.

Fénelon is no less in revolt against Talaeus' theory of delivery. Whereas Talaeus, as we have seen, laid down rules of oral presentation for the speaker to follow, and made these rules the second of the two parts of rhetoric, Fénelon ignores the rules altogether and discusses the principle

[92] See below, p. 63.

upon which they rest, implying meanwhile that they have given the French pulpit a generation of declaimers. He has *A* give *B* the following advice:

The entire art of the good orator consists only in observing what nature does when she is not hampered. Do not do what bad speakers do in striving always to declaim and never to talk to their listeners. On the contrary, each one of your listeners must suppose that you are speaking particularly to him. There you have what produces natural, familiar, and suggestive tones.[93]

Similar considerations are involved in the theory of gesture. Remarking that people do not make many gestures when they are saying unpretentious things, *A* adds:

It would then be necessary either not to make them [*i.e.*, gestures] at all under similar circumstances in a public speech, or to make very few of them; for everything the speaker does ought to follow nature.[94]

And later *A* says this:

The more the action and the voice appear simple and familiar in the places where you are only seeking to instruct, to report, and to suggest, the better do they prepare for surprise and emotion in those places where they are elevated by sudden enthusiasm. It is a kind of music: all its beauty consists in the variety of its tones as they rise or fall according to the things which they have to express.[95]

In his discussion of rhetorical arrangement, Fénelon attacks conceptions which everywhere remind us of Ramus' theory of method. It should in fairness to Ramus be remarked once more that he advocated in the prudential method a looser and more relaxed pattern of organization than in the natural method; but the rigid requirements of the latter, as exemplified in his famous *Dialectique*, became for his followers the laws for method in general. Arnauld, as we have seen, thought it a needless torment for the Ramists to insist that all divisions of discourse have only two members. In actual fact some who wrote in the atmosphere of Ramus' theory recommended even more fantastic

[93] See below, p. 104. [94] See below, p. 100. [95] See below, p. 102.

torments. Thus John Prideaux, an English bishop, taught that preachers undertaking to build sermons upon characterizations, antitheses, or parallels, should cast them into "heptades"—that is, into seven members.[96] With such rigid and artificial arrangements of subject matter Fénelon will have nothing to do. In the early stages of the *Dialogues B* praises the Ash Wednesday sermon for its happy division into three antitheses.[97] Later *A* describes the current theory behind such divisions as "a rather modern invention which comes to us from scholastic philosophy,"[98] and he condemns these divisions as follows:

Ordinarily they put there [*i.e.*, in a discourse] the kind of order that is more apparent than real. Moreover, they dry up the discourse and make it rigid. They cut it into two or three parts, and these hinder the speaker's delivery and the effect delivery ought to produce. No longer is there genuine unity—there are two or three distinct discourses unified only by arbitrary interconnection. Day-before-yesterday's sermon, yesterday's sermon, and today's sermon, provided that they be planned consecutively, as in Advent, make as much of a unity and a living whole together as the three points of one of these sermons make when they are put together.[99]

The theory of arrangement accepted by *A* is discussed at some length soon after he utters the words just quoted.[100] But perhaps a much earlier remark of his will give us in few words Fénelon's essential view:

When you divide, it is necessary to divide simply, naturally. One must have a division that is found ready-made in the very subject itself; a division that clarifies, that puts the materials into classes, that is easily remembered, and that helps one to retain everything else; a division, in short, that reveals the size of the subject and of its parts.[101]

Once a minister has given himself the discipline that produces a simple and natural order in his materials, he does not, as *C* says later, have to spend his life in his study "rounding out periods, retouching portraitures, and contriving rhetorical divisions."[102] Nor does he need to feel,

[96] J. Prideaux, *Sacred Eloquence*, London, 1659, pp. 106-34.
[97] See below, p. 58.   [98] See below, p. 112.   [99] See below, p. 111.
[100] See below, pp. 111-114.   [101] See below, p. 61.   [102] See below, p. 140.

adds *A*, that he must always reduce his eulogies upon the life of a saint to a single point. "It is a scholastic subtlety," *A* continues, "and an indication that an orator is a long way from understanding nature, to have him want to attribute everything to one cause."[103]

Fénelon's hostility to the doctrine of places as an element in invention is even stronger than that of Arnauld in *The Port Royal Logic* or of Lamy in *De L'Art de Parler*. Not only does Fénelon believe this doctrine to be of little value; he omits the explanation of it, and advocates instead a thorough and systematic knowledge of the field in which the speaker's subjects fall. *C* and *A* state these views on more than one occasion. For example, after *A* had dwelt upon the knowledge expected of orators by Plato and Cicero, *C* observes with some wit:

Actually I have noticed on enough occasions that what certain otherwise talented speakers lack most is depth of knowledge. Their minds seem empty. You see that they have been put to no end of trouble to find the wherewithal to piece out their speeches. It even seems that they are not speaking because they are overflowing with truths, but that they are seeking for truths because they are overflowing with a desire to speak.[104]

These words give *A* the opportunity to condemn the traditional doctrine of the places and to mention its proper substitute. He remarks:

You must spend many years in getting abundant resources. After this sort of general preparation, immediate preparations cost little. But if you have only applied yourself to the preparation of particular subjects, you are reduced to paying off in the currency of aphorisms and antitheses; you treat only the commonplaces; you utter nothing but incoherencies; you sew up rags not made for each other; you do not show the real principles of things; you are restricted to superficial and often false arguments; you are incapable of showing the full extent of truth, because all general truths have necessary interconnections, and it is obligatory to know almost all of them in order to handle adequately a particular one.[105]

[103] See below, p. 152.   [104] See below, p. 84.
[105] See below, p. 85.

41

A little later *C* is reminded of the actual application of these comments to the contemporary pulpit. He says:

All this puts me in mind of a preacher, a friend of mine, who lives, as you have it, from day to day. He does not ponder anything until he is scheduled to preach upon it. Then he closes himself in his study, thumbs his concordance, his Combéfis, his *Polyanthea*, some sermon books he has bought, and various collections he has made of purple patches wrested from their context and hit upon by good luck.[106]

Now that the *Dialogues* have been examined as a counterpoise to the theories of Ramus and Talaeus in respect to invention, arrangement, style, and delivery, and have in passing been considered as a reinforcement of Arnauld's reform of method and invention, the task of relating them to their times is almost completed. But it is interesting, before we leave the subject of Arnauld and Fénelon, to observe a few additional similarities between the *Dialogues* and *The Port Royal Logic*. One similarity is that both works emphasize the closeness of the connection between rhetoric and logic. Whereas Arnauld thinks the two subjects to be so closely connected that sound principles of persuasion are not out of place in logic, Fénelon thinks the two subjects to be so closely connected that the obligation to prove by logic is a part of the problem of achieving eloquence.[107] Another similarity is that both works emphasize the necessity of vivid portraiture as an element of effective expression. When Arnauld says, for example, "but the principal design [of eloquence] consists in conceiving things strongly and in expressing them so that one carries over to the minds of the auditors a lively and shining image of them, an image which does not stop at picturing things in a naked way but which also pictures the impulses which one conceives them as having,"[108] he seems to have anticipated almost the very words used by Fénelon in explaining the necessity of portraiture in eloquence. Fénelon thus describes portraiture in poetry and in painting:

106 See below, p. 86.
107 See above, pp. 30-32; see below, pp. 88-90, 92, 95.
108 *Œuvres de Arnauld*, vol. 41, p. 341. Translation mine.

Both the one and the other assume the duty of carrying objects over into the imagination of men.[109]

A little later, comparing poetry and eloquence, Fénelon says:

It is necessary not only to acquaint the listeners with the facts, but to make the facts visible to them, and to strike their consciousness by means of a perfect representation of the arresting manner in which the facts have come to pass.[110]

Still another similarity, and perhaps the most striking of all, is that both works emphasize the relations of the logical and the aesthetic dimensions in an act of literary evaluation. We have remarked already that Arnauld considered it one of the most important rules of true rhetoric never to take as beautiful that which is false. We have seen that Lamy emphasized this same doctrine. Fénelon also states it early in the *Dialogues*. After *A* has pointed out that, despite its "beauties" of style, the Ash Wednesday sermon has an inappropriate text, a text, that is, which does not mean what Ash Wednesday means, *C* remarks, "As for myself, I wish to know whether things are true before I find them beautiful."[111] No other explicit statement in the whole range of the *Dialogues* serves better than this as the central rule of Fénelon's conception of rhetoric. The fact that the same rule was of equal importance in Arnauld's conception of rhetoric suggests an informed interest on the part of Fénelon in the work of his older contemporary.

French writers of the late seventeenth century, like Arnauld, Lamy, and Fénelon, were not the only ones who saw the inadequacies in the system of Ramus and Talaeus and who sought remedies by devising a more flexible and more practical theory of communication. In England there was a similar movement at the same time. For example, in the year 1678, just before Fénelon is believed to have composed his *Dialogues*, Joseph Glanvill, an Englishman, published at London *An Essay concerning Preaching*. This essay condemns ornament, novelty, and patchwork learning in pul-

[109] See below, p. 93.   [110] See below, p. 93.   [111] See below, p. 60.

43

pit oratory, and advocates plain, practical, methodical, and
affectionate sermons. There is a close affinity between Glanvill and Fénelon, even though they were in all probability
unknown to each other. Another work by Glanvill, *A Seasonable Defense of Preaching*, also published at London in
1678, has one characteristic that shows its author to have
been almost the alter ego of Fénelon. The *Seasonable De-
fence* is in the form of a dialogue, with the speakers designated by the symbols *A*, *B*, *C*, *D*, and *E*, the chief spokesman
being *A*. Glanvill's dialogue, however, is conducted by lay-
men, who discuss whether or not preaching is outmoded in
the modern church, and who make historically valuable
comments upon such questions as that of the relative merits
of preaching in the established church and the non-con-
formist sects. In short, Glanvill's subject matter does not
parallel Fénelon's, except that both authors are interested
in plain, forthright, and devoted preaching, the one as an
Anglican who had once been a Puritan, the other as a Catholic who was to have practical experience in converting
Protestants to his faith.

In the long perspective of history, Fénelon's *Dialogues on
Eloquence* appear not only as an effective counterstand
against Ramus' neo-scholastic theory of communication but
also as the first modern rhetoric. It may seem inconsistent
to stress the modernity of the *Dialogues* after saying that
they are directed against Ramus and that they derive their
basic principles from Plato, Cicero, and Saint Augustine.
But in actual fact these judgments do not contradict each
other. Ancient rhetoric is a mixture of brilliant insights and
patiently elaborated routines. The insights have never lost
their value. The elaborate routines, which were devised to
implement the insights and to give man the satisfying illu-
sion that the problems of communication could be solved
by mechanical methods, have proved less durable. Plato's
Phaedrus as a whole and Aristotle's *Rhetoric* in large part
were devoted to the statement of insights into the nature
and method of discourse. The young Cicero in *De Inventione* and his unknown contemporary who wrote the *Rhe-*

torica ad Herennium were beguiled by the elaborate routines which post-Aristotelian rhetoricians had devised.
Later in his life, Cicero reflected in *De Oratore* his growing
interest in the insights of Plato and Aristotle, his diminish-
ing interest in the routines that had appealed to his youth.
Saint Augustine, brought up amidst those routines, especially that which created a machinery for ornamental rhetoric, came at length to feel them inadequate, with the result that the fourth book of his *De Doctrina Christiana*, as
Baldwin has said, "begins rhetoric anew."[112] "It not only
ignores sophistic," adds Baldwin with the same work in
mind, "it goes back over centuries of the lore of personal
triumph to the ancient idea of moving men to truth; and
it gives to the vital counsels of Cicero a new emphasis for
the urgent tasks of preaching the word of God." Like Saint
Augustine, Fénelon began rhetoric anew, not by repudiat-
ing ancient doctrine, but by objecting to the rigid routines
which Ramus had derived from the ancients, and by going
on from there to select from ancient doctrine those insights
which had never lost their modernity. He dealt a severe
blow to the doctrine of places, even as his contemporary
Arnauld had done. He was silent about the lore of tropes
and figures. He stood with Arnauld against the dictum that
patterns of rhetorical arrangement must follow inflexible
rules. He thought of oral delivery as the outward and visible sign of an inward state of conviction and feeling. He
insisted that logic had a place in eloquence, as Arnauld had
insisted that some of the concerns of rhetoric were also concerns of logic. He required, as Arnauld and Plato had done,
that the logical judgment and the aesthetic judgment of
discourse interact upon rather than exclude each other. In
all of these respects he is at once a modern and an ancient,
although there are moderns, as there were ancients, who
accept as valuable the things he ignored or condemned. His
Lettre sur Les Occupations de L'Académie Française, published in 1716, has often been accepted as a better statement
of his entire literary philosophy than are the *Dialogues*.

[112] C. S. Baldwin, *Medieval Rhetoric and Poetic*, New York, 1928, p. 51.

Such a preference is hardly a matter for acrimonious objection. The serious student of Fénelon will read both works. But the *Dialogues* are indisputably the best statement we have of his rhetorical theory, and the earliest statement we have of what may be said to have become the dominant modern attitude towards rhetoric.

IV. THE FRENCH TEXT

THE *Dialogues on Eloquence* have been given many successive editions and printings since their original publication. The first edition appeared at Amsterdam in 1717 and at Paris in 1718 under the editorship of Fénelon's grandnephew, the Marquis of Fénelon, and A. M. Ramsay, the latter of whom supplied the Preface.[113] This edition stands as the best authority for the readings of the text and as the parent of all subsequent editions, the original manuscript having apparently been destroyed or lost before later editors could make use of it.[114] Reproductions of the first edition appeared at Paris in 1740, 1753, and 1774. When Querbeuf edited at Paris between 1787 and 1792 the first "complete" edition of Fénelon's works, the *Dialogues on Eloquence* were put in volume 3 of the 9-volume collection, under the date of 1787. In the same year they were printed at Paris in a single-volume work; and in 1803 at Paris they were twice given a place in publications made up in part of other items. They appeared in 1810 in three forms: 1) at

[113] The first Paris edition has the following title-page: *Dialogues Sur L'Éloquence En Général, Et Sur Celle De La Chaire En Particulier, Avec Une Lettre écrite à l'Académie Françoise.* Par feu Messire François de Salignac de la Motte Fenelon . . . A Paris, chez Florentin Delaulne, ruë S. Jacques, à l'Empereur. M. DCCXVIII. Avec Approbation & Privilege du Roy.

I have not seen a copy of the Amsterdam edition of 1717. It is mentioned, however, by A. Cherel, *Fénelon au XVIIIme siècle en France (Supplément) Tableaux Bibliographiques*, Fribourg, 1917, p. 10.

The royal license under which the first Paris edition was published appears at the end of the volume and assigns publication rights to Jacques Estienne as well as to Delaulne. Copies under the imprint of Estienne are in existence. There is also record of an edition at Amsterdam in 1718; see Cherel, *op. cit.*, p. 11.

[114] Revillout, *op. cit.*, p. 14.

Toulouse as part of volume 3 of the 19-volume reprint of Querbeuf's edition of the "complete" works; 2) at Paris as an item in the 10-volume reprint of the same collection; and 3) at Paris in a single-volume work under the imprint of Mame. Twice in the following year they were printed at Paris in single-volume works.[115] Between 1820 and 1830, Gosselin and Caron edited anew at Versailles and at Paris the complete works of Fénelon in 35 volumes. This collection is for convenience usually called the Versailles edition. According to Carcassonne, it still stands as the best textual authority in the study of Fénelon.[116] The *Dialogues on Eloquence* appear in this edition in volume 21 (1824), page 3 to 121.

The text of the Versailles edition of the *Dialogues* is based upon that of the first Paris edition. But there are discrepancies between the two, some of which increase the utility of the later text, while others do not. On the favorable side, the Versailles edition uses an approximately modern system of spelling and punctuation. Also, in every case but the one to which reference is made in the next footnote, it eliminates the printer's errors listed at the end of the Paris edition. Again, its nineteen references to the source books used by Fénelon outnumber similar references in the Paris edition by six, and are altogether more precise and more helpful to the student. Finally, it contains an improvement over the Paris edition from the reader's point of view—a headnote for each dialogue to indicate its leading ideas. On the less favorable side, there are two criticisms to be leveled against the Versailles edition. One is that on nine occasions it disagrees with the Paris text in identifying the speaker who is doing the talking at that moment, and in only two of these cases, both of which occur in the first half of the first dialogue, does it have any reason to challenge the authority of the older text. The other seven cases, which are to be found at the end of the second and in the

---

[115] For their bibliographical history between 1717 and 1811, I have relied mainly upon Cherel, *op. cit.*, pp. 10, 11, 15, 17, 20, 23, 28, 30, 31.

[116] *État présent des travaux sur Fénelon*, p. 7.

earlier portions of the third dialogue, are witnesses against
the accuracy of the Versailles edition. The other criticism to
be made against it is that its readings conflict with those
of the Paris edition at many places, and in only two or
three of these is there reason to believe that the Versailles
text may be the one to be trusted.[117]

[117] This table shows the major conflicts between the two texts. An asterisk before a reading of the Versailles text indicates that that reading seems preferable to the corresponding one in the Paris text.

PARIS 1718 TEXT	VERSAILLES 1824 TEXT	REFERENCE TO PRESENT TRANSLATION
Le reste du Sermon est du même génie que le texte (p. 10, lines 20-21)	Le reste du sermon est du même genre que le texte (p. 7, lines 30-31)	p. 60, line 33
pour voir que le Poëte (p. 49, lines 8-9)	pour voir que le peintre (p. 26, line 10)	p. 75, line 6
où ils sont amplement (p. 70, lines 20-21)	où ils sont amplement exposés (p. 36, lines 6-7)	p. 82, line 25
du mépris pour ces discours vains (p. 79, lines 2-3; also list of errata, p. 419)	du mépris pour ces discours en l'air (p. 39, lines 31-32)	p. 85, line 32

In the Paris text this line reads originally, "du mépris pour ce discours en l'air." But in the list of errata it is corrected to read "ces discours vains." The Versailles text does not record this correction in full.

je ne rejette que celles où l'Auteur (p. 102, lines 13-14)	je ne rejette que celles où l'orateur (p. 50, lines 26-27)	p. 95, line 22
car j'avois toûjours crû sur l'exemple de *** (p. 109, lines 4-5)	car j'avois toujours cru, sur l'exemple de N... (p. 54, lines 1-2)	p. 98, lines 14-15
il n'est pas même fort instruit (p. 120, lines 7-8)	il n'est pas même fort adroit (p. 59, lines 8-9)	p. 103, lines 30-31
son action est contrainte (p. 134, lines 12-13)	son action est contraire (p. 65, line 25)	p. 109, line 7
je tâcherai pourtant de venir ce soir (pp. 163-64)	*je tâcherai pourtant de venir le soir (p. 79, lines 19-20)	p. 120, lines 6-7

Since the date of its publication, the Versailles text of the *Dialogues* has been often reprinted. I shall not attempt now to list its various printings or comment upon them. The one point to deserve emphasis is that this text, despite its reputation for accuracy, contains several readings which are not in all probability the precise ones originally intended by Fénelon. Thus a translator must use it with caution, although for the general reader it can be recommended as an accessible and substantially correct version of the first Paris edition, which in turn was printed directly from Fénelon's manuscript and editorially supervised by men who knew him intimately.

V. STEVENSON, JENOUR, AND EALES

THERE are three published English translations of the *Dialogues on Eloquence*, in addition to the present one. These require some comment at this juncture.

In the year 1722, only five years after the *Dialogues* first appeared in print, William Stevenson, an English clergyman, published them in their first translation in our language.[118] In a preface entitled "The Translator's Adver-

PARIS 1718 TEXT	VERSAILLES 1824 TEXT	REFERENCE TO PRESENT TRANSLATION
Il est aisé de voir que saint Paul avouë seulement qu'il ne sçait pas bien La Langue Grecque (p. 170, lines 12-15)	Il est aisé de voir que saint Paul avoue qu'il ne sait pas bien la langue grecque (p. 82, lines 25-26)	p. 123, lines 10-12
Selon eux, l'art de l'Eloquence sont les moyens que (p. 178, lines 21-22)	*Selon eux, l'art de l'éloquence consiste dans les moyens que (p. 86, lines 24-25)	p. 126, lines 18-19
de votre Dieu (p. 252, line 18)	de Dieu (p. 121, lines 19-20)	p. 153, line 26

[118] The title-page of the first edition of his translation reads as follows: *Dialogues Concerning Eloquence in General; and particularly, That Kind Which is Fit for the Pulpit: by the Late Archbishop of Cambray. With His Letter to the French Academy, concerning Rhetoric, Poetry, History, and*

tisement," Stevenson offers a general apology for his work; and then he says:

> I have more reason to make some Excuse for the unusual Liberty I have taken in translating the *Dialogues*. 'Tis what I cou'd not avoid. Their Stile is extremely concise; sometimes obscure. And the *Paris*-Edition, (the Standard of the other,) is so faulty, not only in those Places that are mark't among the *unaccurate* ERRATA, but throughout the *Dialogues,* that either they never had the Author's finishing Hand; or they must have been publish't from a very defective Copy. In order therefore to do him justice, I found it necessary to cloath his Thoughts in an *English* Dress, without confining my-self always to a *strict* Translation of the *French*. Accordingly I have paraphras'd several Passages; transpos'd a few; and added whatever seem'd proper to set his true Sentiments in the fullest Light.[119]

Stevenson's translation does not belie his statement of intent. He takes so many liberties with the French text that his work can hardly be accepted as an accurate version.[120] But it does make a genuine effort to annotate Fénelon's references to Cicero, and it has the additional virtue of being the only version generally available to English readers. It appeared at Glasgow in 1750 and 1760; at Leeds in 1806; and in a revised edition at London in 1808. It was given its first American edition at Boston in 1810. It found a place in Ebenezer Porter's *The Young Preacher's Manual, or a Collection of Treatises on Preaching*, published at Boston in 1819 and in a second edition at New York in 1829; in Henry J. Ripley's *Lectures on Systematic Theology and Pulpit Eloquence by the late George Campbell . . . To which are added, Dialogues on Eloquence by M. de Féne-*

---

a Comparison betwixt the Antients and Moderns. Translated from the French, and illustrated with Notes and Quotations; by William Stevenson, M. A. Rector of Morningthorp in Norfolk. London: Printed by T. Wood, for J. Walthoe, Jun. over-against the Royal Exchange in Cornhill. M DCCXXII.

119 Pp. v-vi.

120 The following pages of the first edition of his translation contain passages unauthorized by the French text, or transposed out of their original sequence, or lacking in material found in the French text: 3, 22, 23, 24, 32, 45, 48, 53, 56, 66, 67, 72, 80, 121, 123, 125, 129, 130, 131, 141, 165, 166, 188, 191.

lon, published at Boston in 1832; and in Edwards A. Park's *The Preacher and Pastor*, published at New York in 1845. One or more of these editions can usually be located today in the larger libraries of America and England.

The second English version, published at London in 1847 and reissued there in 1849, was made by Alfred Jenour, minister of Regent Square Chapel;[121] but it apparently did not have a wide circulation, and copies of it are now almost unobtainable. In his Preface, Jenour remarks that the *Dialogues* have been neglected by English readers, perhaps through "want of a readable translation," or because few people read French with zest and interest. Speaking of himself in the third person, he thus describes his aim as translator:

In making the translation, he has not attempted to be literal. His object has been rather to give the matter and spirit of the author, than his words; to express his sentiments, in short, as nearly as possible, in the language which we may conceive Fénelon would have used had he written in English, and in the nineteenth century. Nothing, however, has been added or omitted; the phraseology alone has been changed, and that only when a literal rendering of the French would have sounded tame and feeble.

With these principles one has no reason to quarrel. The trouble is, however, that Jenour's translation does not succeed in following Fénelon's text without omissions and errors.[122] His work, in fact, is careless and amateurish. And his annotations have no value for the student of Fénelon's

[121] The title-page of its first edition reads as follows: *Hints on Preaching: Being Fénelon's Dialogues on Eloquence, Particularly the Eloquence of the Pulpit* Translated from the French, with a Preliminary Essay, having Especial Reference to the Faults of Modern Preachers by the Rev. Alfred Jenour, Minister of Regent Square Chapel, Author of "Commentary on Isaiah," etc. etc., . . . London: T. D. Thomson, 13, Upper King Street, Russell Square. James Nisbet and Co.; Hamilton, Adams, and Co. Edinburgh: W. P. Kennedy, 1847.

[122] On the following pages the first edition has passages that omit parts of the French text, that identify the speakers improperly, or that depart from the meaning of the original: 34, 36, 45, 50, 51, 53, 57, 58, 72, 73, 74, 75, 79, 82, 90, 98, 100, 101, 103, 108, 113, 119, 120, 129, 141, 145, 149, 163, 169, 178, 188.

INTRODUCTION

sources, although they may be of interest to the social historian who is looking for evidence in the nineteenth century of Protestant antagonism towards certain aspects of the doctrine of the Catholic Church.

The third English translation of the *Dialogues*, published fifty years after the one just discussed, is almost completely unavailable to the reader of today. It was the work of Samuel J. Eales, vicar of Stalisfield, Kent.[123] Eales did not mention either of the translations that had preceded his. In his introductory essay he speaks of the importance of preaching and proceeds then to discuss its principles. His final paragraph, referring to points he had made, emphasizes that Fénelon's *Dialogues* promote "this sincerity and depth," "this vital energy and force," "this natural and unsophisticated utterance." As his translation proceeds, it is to be noticed that he, like Stevenson and Jenour, omits portions of the French text and occasionally misconstrues it.[124] His notes are in the main quotations from works on pulpit eloquence to illustrate and support Fénelon's doctrine. Although they have no bearing upon the study of the antecedents of the *Dialogues on Eloquence*, they are of some rhetorical interest. Because of this fact, and because his renderings of the French text are mainly accurate and complete, Eales's work is more deserving of praise than is that of Stevenson or Jenour.

[123] Its title-page reads as follows: *Three Dialogues on Pulpit Eloquence by Mgr. François de Salignac de Lamothe Fénélon Archbishop of Cambrai* Translated and Illustrated by Quotations from Modern Writers with an Introductory Essay by the late Samuel J. Eales, M. A., D. C. L., Vicar of Stalisfield, Kent, Editor and Translator of the Works of S. Bernard; of Bishop Dupanloup's "Ministry of Preaching," Etc. London: Thomas Baker Philadelphia: John J. McVey. 1897.

[124] The following pages of his work afford examples: 8, 14, 20, 43, 52, 55, 60, 80, 113, 114, 118, 133, 141, 174.

At the end of the second and the beginning of the third dialogue, Eales, against the authority of the Versailles text, attempts to force the interpretation that the third dialogue took place in the evening of the day when the second was held, instead of on the day following. He apparently followed the reading "ce soir" of the first Paris edition, p. 164, not the reading "le soir" of the Versailles text, p. 79. The latter reading seems preferable.

VI. THE PRESENT TRANSLATION

THE present translation is based upon the text of the first
Paris edition and of the Versailles edition. The nature of
the disagreements between these two texts has been discussed in an earlier section of this Introduction, and I believe my own procedure in regard to those disagreements is
sufficiently indicated in that discussion.[125] Throughout the
performance of my task as translator, I have tried to safe-
guard myself against inaccuracy by comparing my version to
each of the three English versions just mentioned. Without
this sort of assistance my work would have suffered a distinct
loss. I have striven to protect myself against the omission of
any portion of the French text; against the faulty identification of the speakers; and against the interpretation of the
text in words that are not responsive to the meaning of
Fénelon's rhetorical terminology. In my notes I have en-
deavored to correct inaccuracies in the work of earlier an-
notators, and to provide those additional notes that would
anchor all of Fénelon's borrowings to their exact sources.[126]
I have also given what information I could to help modern
readers understand Fénelon's allusions to his own or earlier
times. I do not assume that I have avoided all pitfalls; but
at least I can say that I have tried to be mindful of most of
them. My hope is that the present translation will serve to
interest students of rhetoric, literary criticism, and aesthet-
ics, no less than preachers, writers, and speakers, in the rhetorical doctrine of a man who discusses with erudition and
eloquence the permanent issues of literary art.

[125] See above, pp. 47-49.
[126] The French edition with the fullest and most helpful notes is that
of E. Despois, *Fénelon. Dialogues sur l'éloquence en général et sur celle de
la chaire en particulier, suivis du Discours de réception à L'Académie
Française*, nouvelle édition, collationnée sur les meilleurs textes et accom-
pagnée de notes historiques, littéraires, et grammaticales, Paris, 1847. Despois, however, does not view all of the errors of the Versailles text, as indicated above, p. 48, note 117, with much suspicion, except at one point,
and there (p. 158 of his edition) he does not confirm his emendation by
recognizing the Paris text as the superior authority.

FENELON'S

DIALOGUES ON ELOQUENCE

The First Dialogue

AGAINST THE AFFECTATION OF FINE WIT IN SERMONS. THE END
OF ELOQUENCE IS TO INSTRUCT MANKIND AND MAKE MEN
BETTER. THE SPEAKER WILL NOT ATTAIN THIS END UNLESS HE
IS FORGETFUL OF SELF-INTEREST.

The speakers are designated by the letters A, B, and C.

A. Well, now, sir, have you just been listening to the
sermon that you wanted to take me to hear? As for myself,
I am perfectly content with the preacher of our own parish.

B. So am I with the one I heard. You have lost, sir, by
not being there. I have engaged a pew in order not to miss
any of his sermons in Lent. He is an admirable man; if you
were to listen to him once, he would make you lose your
appetite for anyone else.

A. Then I shall take good care not to go hear him, for
I do not want a preacher who makes me lose my appetite for
others. On the contrary, I am looking for a man who gives
me such an appetite and such esteem for the word of God
that I may be the more disposed to listen to it everywhere
else. But since I have lost so much and you are so full of
this beautiful sermon, you may, sir, make amends to me.
Pray tell me what you remember of it.

B. I'll ruin the sermon by trying to repeat it—a hundred beauties in it will escape my mind. It would be necessary for me to be the preacher himself in order to tell
you . . .

A. But why? His plan, his arguments, his moral, the
principal truths which made up the body of his discourse—
does nothing of these remain in your mind? Is it that you
were not paying attention?

B. I beg your pardon—I have never been more attentive.

C. What then! Do you wish to be urged?

B. No. Yet his were thoughts so delicate, so dependent
upon the turn and the refinement of the expression, that

they delight you at the moment but are not easily recovered afterwards. Even though you should remember them and should repeat them in other terms, they are not any longer the same thing—they lose their grace and strength.

A. Then, sir, they are very fragile beauties indeed, if in wishing to touch them, you make them disappear. I should prefer a discourse with more body and less spirit—it would make a strong impression, and you would remember it better. Why should you speak if not to persuade, to instruct, and to proceed in such fashion that the listener remembers what you say?

C. There you are, sir. You must answer.

B. Oh well, then, let me tell you what I remember. Here is the text: "Cinerem tamquam panem manduca- bam,"[1] "For I have eaten ashes like bread." Could you find a more ingenious text for Ash Wednesday? He pointed out that, according to this passage, ashes ought today to be the food for our souls. Then he inserted into his introduction, in the most engaging way in the world, the story of Arte- misia[2] and her husband's ashes. His transition to his *Ave Maria* was most skillful. His division of topics was happy— you shall judge of that for yourself. Although these ashes, he said, may be a symbol of punishment, they are a source of congratulation. Although they may seem to abase us, they are a fountainhead of fame. Although they may rep- resent death, they are a medicine that brings immortal life. He repeated that division in many ways, and each time he gave new luster to his antitheses. The rest of the speech was not less polished nor less brilliant: the diction was pure; the thoughts fresh; the periods rhythmical, and each with some surprising stroke at the end. He painted for us moral pictures in which each one of us recognized him- self; he anatomized the passions of the human heart in such

[1] In the Vulgate, *Psalm* 101.10; in the King James Version, *Psalm* 102.9.

[2] Artemisia, wife of Mausolus, king of Caria. Her grief at the death of her husband, which occurred around 352 B.C., led her to build a splendid tomb for him. It was regarded as one of the seven wonders of the ancient world, and it gave the Greek language a word from which our word "mau- soleum" is derived.

a way as to equal the *Maxims* of La Rochefoucauld. To my mind, in sum, it was a perfect speech. What do you think of it, sir?

A. I fear to speak to you about it and to deprive you of the good opinion that you have of it. One ought to respect the word of God, to profit by all the truths which a preacher sets forth, and to avoid a critical attitude, for fear of weakening the authority of the ministry.

B. No, sir, don't be afraid. It is not in curiosity that I ask you. I need to have sound ideas upon this matter. I wish to instruct myself solidly, not only for my own needs, but for those of others, for my profession requires me to preach. Speak to me then without reserve, and do not fear either to contradict or shock me.

A. You wish it, and I must obey you. Judging by your own report of it, I consider that it was a mischievous sermon.

B. How so?

A. You are going to see why. A sermon in which there are false applications of the Scripture, in which a secular story is told in a cold and childish manner, and in which you see reigning throughout a vain affectation of wit—is that, then, a good sermon?

B. No, certainly not. But the sermon I reported to you does not seem to me to be of that sort.

A. Wait; you will agree with what I say. When the preacher chose for his text the words, "For I have eaten ashes like bread," ought he to have contented himself merely with finding a verbal affinity between that text and today's ceremony? Should he not have begun by understanding the true sense of the text before he applied it to his subject?

B. Yes indeed.

A. Should he not then have carried things back much farther, and have sought to enter into the meaning of the whole psalm? Would it not have been proper for him to determine whether the interpretation with which he was

59

dealing was contrary to the true meaning, before he gave it to the people as the word of God?

B. That is right. But in what respect can it be contrary?

A. David or whoever else may be the author of *Psalm* 101 speaks there of his misfortunes. He says that his enemies, seeing him in the dust, struck down at their feet, grinded (this is here a poetical expression) into nourishing himself upon the bread of ashes and a drink mingled with tears, cruelly mocked him. What connection is there between the lament of David, wrenched from his throne and persecuted by his son Absalom, and the humility of a Christian who puts ashes upon his forehead to remind himself of death and to disengage himself from the pleasures of this world? Did he not have another text in the Scripture that he might have taken? Jesus Christ, the apostles, the prophets—did they never speak of death and the ashes of the grave, to which God reduces our vanity? Is not the Scripture full of a thousand moving images that bear upon this truth? Are not the very words of *Genesis*,[3] so apt, so natural to this ceremony, and chosen by the church herself, worthy of the choice of a preacher? Should he fear in false nicety to repeat too often a text which the Holy Ghost and the church have wished to be repeated each year forever? Why then should he ignore this suitable passage, and so many others in the Scripture, in order to find one which is not suitable? His is a depraved taste, a blind enthusiasm to say something new.

B. You speak too warmly, sir; but it is true that this text is not suitable according to its literal interpretation.

C. As for myself, I wish to know whether things are true before I find them beautiful. But what of the rest?

A. The rest of the sermon is in the same vein as the text. Don't you see this, sir? Why seek the pleasant in a subject so terrifying? And why amuse the listener by a secular story of the grief of Artemisia, when one ought to thunder and present only the terrible images of death?

[3] 3.19.

B. I see that you don't like flashes of wit. But without that attraction, what would become of eloquence? Do you wish to limit all preachers to the simplicity of missionaries? Simplicity is necessary for the common people; but gentlemen have more refined ears, and one must adjust oneself to their taste.

A. That is another matter. I meant to finish showing you how badly this sermon is conceived. It only remained for me to speak of the division of topics, but I think you yourself know well enough what makes me disapprove of that. Here is a man who gives three points as the subject of his entire discourse. When you divide, it is necessary to divide simply, naturally. One must have a division that is found ready-made in the very subject itself; a division that clarifies, that puts the materials into classes, that is easily remembered, and that helps one to retain everything else; a division, in short, that reveals the size of the subject and of its parts. But you see here a man who undertakes first to bedazzle you, who retails to you three epigrams or three riddles, who turns and twists them subtly—you think you are seeing sleight of hand. Is there in such things the serious and grave mien suited to making you expect something useful and important? But let us come back to what you said. You asked if I wish, then, to banish eloquence from the pulpit?

B. Yes. It seems to me that you are headed in that direction.

A. Ah, we shall see. What is eloquence?

B. It is the art of speaking well.

A. Has this art no other aim than that of speaking well? When men speak, have they not some purpose? Do they speak only to speak?

B. No, they speak in order to please and to persuade.

A. If you please, sir, let us carefully distinguish these two things. They speak to persuade—that is what they always do. They also speak to please—that is merely what they too often do. But when they seek to please, they have another, a more distant, aim, which is nevertheless the principal one. The good man seeks to please only that he may urge justice and the other virtues by making them attractive. He who seeks his own interest, his reputation, his fortune, dreams of pleasing only that he may gain the bow and esteem of men able to satisfy his greed or his ambition. Thus, even his case can be reduced like that of the good man to persuasion as the single aim which a speaker has; for the self-interested man wishes to please in order to flatter, and he flatters in order to inculcate that which suits his interest.

B. In sum, it is impossible for you to deny that men sometimes speak merely in order to please. The pagan orators had this aim. It is easy to see in the speeches of Cicero that he strove for his own reputation. Who would not believe the same thing of Isocrates and Demosthenes? All the ancient eulogists meant less to make their great men esteemed than to make themselves admired. They only sought to glorify a prince because of that glory which would have to return to themselves if they celebrated his well. At all times among the Greeks and the Romans, such ambitions appear to have been permissible. By competition of this sort, eloquence was perfected, and minds were raised to high thoughts and great passions. One comes to see that the ancient republics flourished by such means. The pomp which inspired eloquence, and the power which she had over the people, rendered her admirable and marvelously refined the human spirit. I do not see why you should condemn that competition, even among Christian speakers, provided that no indecent affectation appear in their discourses, and that they do not weaken in any way the lesson of the Gospels. It is pointless to condemn something which attracts young men and makes great preachers.

A. Here are a goodly number of things, sir, that you have lumped together. Let us disentangle them, if you please, and see in an orderly way what ought to be inferred from them. Above all, let us avoid the spirit of dispute; let us examine this matter calmly, like men who only fear falsehood; and let us find every honor in retracting our statements as soon as we see that we have been misled.

B. I am in the same mood, or at least I believe I am; and you will give me pleasure if you notify me whenever you see that I am departing from this rule.

A. Let us not speak first of preachers. They will appear in due time. Let us begin with secular speakers, of whom you have just cited an example. You have put Demosthenes with Isocrates. In that, you have done wrong to the former. The latter is a lifeless speaker who meant only to polish his thoughts and to give melody to his utterances. He had but a low conception of eloquence, and he reduced it almost entirely to the arrangement of words. A man who according to some took ten years, and according to others, fifteen, to arrange the periods of his Panegyric,[4] which is a speech on the needs of Greece, was of feeble and belated assistance to the republic against the enterprises of the king of Persia. Demosthenes spoke quite otherwise against Philip. You can look at the comparison which Dionysius of Halicarnassus made of the two speakers, and at the essential faults which he detects in Isocrates.[5] You only see in Isocrates a flowery and effeminate discourse, and periods contrived with infinite labor to please the ear, while Demosthenes moves, warms, and captivates the heart. He is too keenly engaged with the interests of his country to amuse himself with all the conceits of Isocrates. His is an argument tight and urgent, his the liberal feelings of a soul which conceives nothing but the great, his a discourse which grows and supports itself at each word by new proofs, his a chain of bold and striking figures. You do not know how to read him without seeing that he carries the republic in the depth of his heart. It is nature herself who speaks in his ecstasy—the art is so perfect that it does not appear anywhere—nothing ever equaled his rapidity and vehemence. Have you ever looked

[4] See Plutarch, *De Gloria Atheniensium*, 8 (350E); see also Longinus, *On the Sublime*, Sec. 4, and Quintilian, *Institutio Oratoria*, 10.4.4.

[5] See Dionysius of Halicarnassus, *De Admiranda Vi Dicendi in Demosthene*, chs. 16-36.

at what Longinus said of him in his treatise *On the Sublime?*

B. No. Isn't it that treatise which Boileau translated? Is it good?

A. I do not fear to say that to my mind it surpasses Aristotle's *Rhetoric.* Although very good, the *Rhetoric* contains many dry precepts—precepts which are more curious than useful in practice. Thus it serves rather better to bring the rules of art to the notice of those who are already eloquent than to inspire eloquence and form true speakers. But the *Sublime* of Longinus ties to precepts the very examples to make them clear. This author treats the sublime in a sublime way, as the translator expresses it. He warms the imagination, he elevates the spirit of the reader, he forms the reader's taste, and teaches him judiciously to distinguish the good and the bad in the celebrated speakers of antiquity.

B. What! Longinus so admirable! Ha! Did he not live at the time of the Emperor Aurelian and of Zenobia?

A. Yes, you know their story.

B. Was not that age pretty far below the refinement of preceding ages? What! Would you have it that an author of that time had better taste than Isocrates? In truth, I can't believe it.

A. I have been surprised at it myself. But you only have to read him. Though he lived in a completely corrupted century, he had been bred upon the ancients, and he keeps hardly a trace of the defects of his time. I say, hardly a trace, because it is necessary to acknowledge that he applied himself more to the admirable than to the useful, and that he scarcely connected eloquence and morality. In these regards he appears not to have the solid views that the ancient Greeks, especially the philosophers, had. Yet even so, you must pardon him for this deficiency, in respect to which Isocrates, although of a better century, was greatly inferior to him. This deficiency is particularly excusable in a private work, where Longinus is speaking not of that which instructs men but of that which beguiles and impresses them. I speak to you of this author because he will serve above all to make you understand what I wish to say: you will see there the admirable portrait he draws of Demosthenes, whose sublimest passages he quotes; and you will also find there what I have said about the defects of Isocrates.[6] You could not possibly take a better road to a knowledge of these two authors, unless you wish to take the pains to know them directly by reading their own works. Now let us leave Isocrates and return to Demosthenes and Cicero.

B. You leave Isocrates because he embarrasses you.

A. Then let us speak again of Isocrates, since you are unconvinced. Let us judge his eloquence by the very rules of eloquence, and by the opinion of the most eloquent writer of antiquity—Plato. Will you trust him in this, sir?

B. I'll trust him if he's right. I do not take for granted the word of any master.

A. Keep that rule in mind; it is all that I ask. Provided that you do not let yourself be dominated by certain prejudices of our time, reason will soon convince you. Do not trust Isocrates or Plato in this matter, but judge the one and the other by self-evident principles. You could not deny that the aim of eloquence is to persuade men to truth and virtue.

B. I do not agree. That is what I have already denied.

A. Then that is what I'm going to prove to you. Eloquence, if I do not fool myself, can be taken as three things: 1) as the art of persuading men of the truth and making them better; 2) as a neutral art which the mischievous as well as the good can make use of, and which can enforce falsehood and injustice no less than justice and truth; 3) and lastly, as an art which selfish men can use in order to give pleasure, to acquire a reputation, and to make their fortune. Grant one of these three kinds, will you?

B. I grant them all. What do you make of that?

A. Wait, what follows will show you that. Be satisfied

[6] See Longinus, *On the Sublime*, Secs. 2, 4, 10, 12, 15, 16, 17, 18, 20, 21, 24, 27, 32, 34, 38, 39.

that I do not say anything to you but what is clear, and that I get you to see my point. Of these three kinds of eloquence, you would doubtless approve of the first.

B. Yes, that is the best.

A. And the second, what do you think of it?

B. I see your drift. You are planning a sophistry. The second is reprehensible by reason of the evil application which the speaker makes of eloquence in enforcing injustice and falsehood. The eloquence of a mischievous man is good in itself; but the end with which he connects it is dangerous. Now we ought to speak of the rules of eloquence, and not of the application which it is possible to make of them. Let us not, if you please, get away from what our real question is.

A. You will see that I am not getting away from it, if you really wish to continue to listen to me sympathetically. You condemn the second kind, then; or, to avoid any equivocation, you condemn eloquence put to this second use.

B. Good, you say it exactly. We're completely agreed.

A. And the third use of eloquence, which is to seek to please by language in order to gain reputation and fortune—what do you say of it?

B. You already know my opinion; I haven't changed it. This use of eloquence seems fair to me. It stimulates rivalry and perfects men's minds.

A. In what direction would you try to perfect men's minds? If you had to organize a state or a republic, in what would you wish to perfect the citizens' minds?

B. In all those ways that might make them better. I would wish to fashion good citizens, full of zeal for the public good. I would wish them to know how to defend their country in war, how to make the laws observed in peace, how to manage their homes, cultivate or supervise the cultivation of their farms, educate their children in virtue and inspire them in religion, engage in commerce as the needs of the country dictate, and apply themselves to the sciences useful to life. This seems to me the aim of a lawmaker.

A. Your views are very just and sound. Then you would

66

wish citizens to dislike idleness and to be occupied with very serious matters and to strive always towards the public good?

B. Yes indeed.

A. And you would curtail all other things?

B. I would curtail them.

A. You would only allow bodily exercises for health and strength? I do not speak of beauty of body because that is a natural result of health and strength in well-formed bodies.

B. I would allow only such exercises.

A. Then you would curtail all those which served merely to amuse, and which did not put men in condition to support well the prescribed activities of peace and the fatigues of war?

B. Yes, I would follow that rule.

A. It is no doubt by the same rule that you would also curtail (for you have told me as much) all exercises of the mind which would not serve to make the soul healthy, strong, and beautiful as it became virtuous?

B. I agree to that. What follows from it? I do not see any more where you are headed, your way is so roundabout.

A. It is that I wish to find first principles and to leave behind me nothing of doubt. Please answer.

B. I say that, having established that rule for the body, you have a much stronger reason to follow it for the soul.

A. You would not permit any of the sciences or any of the arts which serve only for pleasure, for amusement, and for curiosity? What would become of those which belonged neither to the tasks of domestic life nor to the duties of public life?

B. I would banish them from my republic.

A. Then if you permitted mathematicians, it would be on account of mechanics, navigation, surveying of territories, the computations which must be made, the fortifications of places, etc. These are the employments which authorize them. If you admitted physicians and lawyers, it would be to preserve health and justice. It would be the same for other professions which we feel the need of. But what would you do with musicians? Would you not agree with those ancient Greeks who never separated the useful from the pleasant? The Greeks, who developed music and poetry, united as one, to so high a perfection, intended that these should serve to ennoble the heart and to inspire great passions. It was by music and poetry that they prepared themselves for battle; they took musicians and musical instruments to war. In line with this came also the trumpets and drums to stir them to an enthusiasm and a sort of madness which they called divine. It was by music and the cadence of verse that they softened ferocious tribes. It was by this harmony that they instilled wisdom along with pleasure into the depths of their children's hearts. They made them sing Homer's verse in order to inspire them in an agreeable way with a contempt for death, for riches, and for the pleasures which weaken the soul; and to stir them to the love of glory, liberty, and native land. Even their dances had a serious aim in their way, and it is certain that they did not dance solely for pleasure. We see by the example of David that oriental peoples regarded dancing as a serious art, analogous to music and poetry. A thousand precepts were mingled in their fables and poems; thus the gravest and most austere philosophy showed itself only with a laughing face. This appeared again in the priest's mysterious dances, which the pagans mingled with their ceremonies for the festivals of the gods. All the arts which consist in melodious sounds, or in movements of the body, or in the use of language—in a word, music, dancing, eloquence, poetry—were devised only to express the passions and to inspire them in the very act of expressing them. By such means as these, mankind wished to impress great thoughts upon the human soul and to bring to men lively and striking pictures of the beauty of virtue and the ugliness of evil. Thus all these arts appeared to be for pleasure, but were in reality among the ancients a part of their deepest striving for morality and religion. Even the chase was an apprenticeship for war. Pleasures the most attractive contained some virtuous lesson. From that source there came to Greece so many heroic virtues, admired by all ages. This first system of education was changed, it is true, and it had indeed its own extreme defects. Its essential defect was that it was founded upon a false and dangerous religion. In that respect, the Greeks were deceived, as were all the wise men of a world then plunged in idolatry; but if they deceived themselves in the foundation of religion and in the choice of leading truths, they did not deceive themselves about the way to inculcate religion and virtue. In that respect, all was concrete, pleasant, fitted to make a lively impression.

C. You just said that this first system of education was changed. Please do not forget to explain that to us.

A. Yes, it was changed. Virtue gives true refinement. But soon, if you do not guard against it, refinement degenerates little by little. The Asiatic Greeks were the first to be corrupted; the Ionians became effeminate;[7] all that coast of Asia became a playhouse of luxury. Crete, despite the wise laws of Minos, was likewise corrupted—you know the verses which Saint Paul quotes.[8] Corinth was notorious for her luxury and her dissipations. The Romans, still half-civilized, began to find ways to weaken their rustic virtue. Athens was not immune to this contagion; all Greece was infected with it. Pleasure, which ought only to be the means to inculcate wisdom, usurped the place of wisdom herself. The philosophers protested. Socrates arose and demonstrated to his misled fellow citizens that the pleasure which they made their goal ought only to be the highway to virtue. Plato, his disciple, who was not ashamed to compose his writings out of the conversations of his master, excludes from his republic every note of music, every appeal of tragedy, every recital of poems, and even the passages of Homer, that did not go to inspire the love of good laws.[9] There you

7 Horace, *Odes*, 3.6.21.

8 *Titus*, 1.12.

9 Plato, *Republic*. For those passages in which Plato discusses the matters referred to here, see Lane Cooper, *Plato Phaedrus, Ion, Gorgias, and Symposium, with passages from the Republic and Laws*, New York, Oxford University Press, 1938, pp. 282-360.

have the judgment which Socrates and Plato pronounce upon the poets and musicians. Are you not of their opinion?

B. I share their sentiments exactly. Man should not tolerate anything that is useless. Since he can find pleasure in serious things, he does not have to seek it elsewhere. If anything can assist the cause of virtue, the identification of virtue with pleasure can do so. On the contrary, when you separate them, you strongly invite men to abandon virtue. Besides, everything that pleases without instructing beguiles and softens merely. Ha! Do you not find that I am becoming a philosopher in listening to you? But let us go on to the end, for we are not as yet in agreement.

A. We will be soon, sir. Since you are so much the philosopher, permit me again to ask you a question. Here are musicians and poets restricted only to inspiring virtue; here are the citizens of your republic barred from plays in which pleasure is without precept. But what will you do with the soothsayers?

B. They are impostors; they must be chased out.

A. But they do not work evil. You know well that they are not sorcerers. Thus it is not the devil's art that you fear in them.

B. No, I don't bother to fear that, for I don't put the least bit of faith in all their stories; but they do enough mischief by amusing the public. I shall not permit in my republic the idle gentry who amuse others and have no other occupation but that of talking.

A. But they earn their living by that means. They earn money for themselves and their families.

B. No matter. Let them earn their living in some other way. It is not only necessary to earn a living, but it is also necessary to earn it by occupations useful to the public. I would say the same thing to all those vagabonds who amuse the passers-by with their prattle and their songs. When they never lie, when they say nothing dishonest, it will be necessary even so to chase them out—their uselessness alone suffices to make them guilty. The police ought to force them to take some regular occupation.

A. But would you allow those who act in tragedies? That is, assuming that there is nothing of secular love nor of immodesty mixed in with these plays. Moreover, I do not speak now as a Christian. Reply only as a legislator and philosopher.

B. If these tragedies do not have the purpose of instructing while giving pleasure, I would ban them.

A. Good. Now you are precisely of Plato's opinion, who will not permit in his republic poems and tragedies that have not been examined by the guardians of the laws, to the end that the people will never see or hear anything which does not serve to strengthen the laws and to inspire to virtue. Now also you follow the spirit of the ancient authors, who preferred that tragedy should revolve upon two passions: namely, fear, which the destructive results of evil ought to arouse; and pity, which a persecuted and patient virtue inspires. Such is the conception which Euripides and Sophocles carried out.[10]

B. You remind me that I have read that latter rule in Boileau's *Art of Poetry*.

A. You're right. There is a man who well knows not only the basis of poetry but also the solid goal towards which philosophy, the superior of all the arts, should guide the poet.

B. But I say, where are you taking me now?

A. I am not taking you anywhere. You are walking quite alone. Here you are happily arrived at the goal. Have you not said that you would not allow in your republic the idle gentry who amuse others and have no other occupation than that of talking? Is it not on this principle that you have expelled all those who act in tragedies in which instruction is not mingled with pleasure? Will you permit to be done in prose that which you will not permit in verse? After so much severity, how could you be indulgent towards the declaimers who speak only to show their fine wit?

B. But the declaimers of whom we are speaking have two praiseworthy aims.

10 See also Aristotle, *Poetics*, chs. 6, 9, 13, 14.

A. Explain them.

B. The first aim is that of working for themselves. By this means they achieve honorable positions. Eloquence produces reputation, and reputation brings with it the fortune that they need.

A. You yourself have already replied to your own objection. Did you not say that it was necessary not only to earn a living but to earn it by occupations useful to the public? He who acts in tragedies which involve nothing in the way of instruction earns a living. That consideration, however, does not hinder you from excluding him from your republic. You would say to him: "Take a substantial and prescribed occupation; don't entertain the citizenry. If you wish to get a legitimate profit from them, work towards some positive good, or towards making them good." Why will you not say the same thing to the speaker?

B. There we are agreed. Their second aim, which I wish to tell you of, explains all that.

A. How? Then give it, please.

B. It is that the speaker works also for the public.

A. In what way?

B. He refines men's minds. He teaches them eloquence.

A. Wait. If I invent a fantastic art or an imaginary language, from which no one can derive the least advantage, would it be a service to the public to teach them that art or language?

B. No, because you only serve others in proportion as you teach them something useful.

A. Then you could not convincingly prove that a speaker serves the public by teaching them eloquence, if you have not already proved that the eloquence itself serves some purpose. For what do a man's beautiful speeches serve, if fine as they are they contribute no benefit whatever to the public?[11] Words are made for men, as Saint Augustine says,[12] and not men for words. As I well know, speeches serve

---

[11] St. Augustine, *De Doctrina Christiana*, 4.10.24.

[12] *De Doctrina Christiana*, 4.28.61. St. Augustine's words are: "nec doctor verbis serviat, sed verba doctori."

him who makes them; for they dazzle the listeners, they
create much talk about him who makes them, and some
people even have the bad taste to give him money for his
useless words. But should an eloquence that is mercenary
and of no benefit to the public be suffered in the state which
you control? A shoemaker at least makes shoes and supports
his family only by money earned in ministering to the actual needs of the public. Thus, you see, the meanest occupations have a solid aim; and the art of the speaker alone
has no aim but to entertain men with talk! Its whole aim,
that is, boils down to satisfying the curiosity and whiling
away the idleness of the listener, on the one hand, and to
gratifying the vanity and the ambition of him who speaks,
on the other. In the good name of your republic, sir, do not
permit such an abuse.

B. Oh, well. I recognize that the speaker's aim must be
to instruct and to make men better.

A. Keep clearly in mind what you have just now admitted—you will see the consequences of it.

B. But they do not create such an obstacle that a man
who labors to instruct others could not be quite delighted
at the same time to acquire reputation and wealth.

A. We still are not speaking here as Christians. I need
philosophy alone against you. I repeat then that speakers,
according to you, are the sort who must instruct other men
and make them better than they are. There as a first result
you have eliminated the declaimers. It is not even possible
for you to allow eulogists, except so far as they set forth
models worthy of being imitated, and so far as they make
virtue attractive by their praises.

B. What! Is a eulogy worth nothing, then, if it is not
brimming with morality?

A. Isn't that your very own conclusion? A man must
speak only to instruct. He must praise the great only in
order that he may teach their virtues to the people, in order
that he may induce the people to imitate them, in order that he may show glory and virtue to be inseparable.
Thus it is necessary to exclude from a eulogy all vague, ex-

cessive, and fawning praise; and to leave there not one of the sterile thoughts that carry no instruction to the listener. It must be that every word of it tends to make the listener love virue. But eulogists for the most part appear not to praise the virtues except to praise the men who practiced them—and for whom they have undertaken the eulogy. Suppose we have to praise a man. The eulogists emphasize above all other virtues those which he has practiced. But everything has its turn. On another occasion they talk down the virtues which they had talked up, in favor of some other man whom they would flatter. It is by this principle that I condemn Pliny.[13] If he had praised Trajan in order to mold other great men to the form of that one, his would have been an insight worthy of a speaker. Great as he is, Trajan ought not to have been the goal of Pliny's speech. Trajan ought to be only an example set forth to invite men to be virtuous. When a eulogist merely has the base aim of praising a particular man, his is nothing more than the flattery that speaks to vanity.

B. But what would you say about the poems written to praise great men? Homer has his Achilles, Virgil his Aeneas. Do you mean to condemn these two poets?

A. No, sir. But you have only to examine the intent of their poems. In the *Iliad*, Achilles is in truth the leading hero; but the praise of him is not the principal object of the poem. He is represented naturally with all his faults; these faults, indeed, are one of the subjects upon which the poet sought to instruct posterity. He tries in that work to inspire in the Greeks the love of glory that you earn in combat, and fear of the disunion that stands as the barrier to every conspicuous success. This moral aim is seen openly throughout the poem. It is true that the *Odyssey* pictures Ulysses as a steadier and more perfect hero; but that is a chance effect, and means only that a man like Ulysses, whose characteristic is wisdom, would have a more correct and

---

[13] Pliny the Younger (A.D. 61?-113?), best known for his *Letters*, was also the author of many speeches, his *Panegyric on Trajan* being the only one now extant. For Pliny's own account of this speech, see his *Letters*, 3.18.

more consistent behavior than that of a young man with the hot and impetuous disposition of an Achilles. Thus in the one as in the other case Homer intended only to paint nature faithfully. Over and above this, the *Odyssey* throughout contains a thousand moral counsels for every detail of life; and it is necessary merely to read it to see that the poet has painted a wise man who gets through everything by his wisdom, and has painted him only to show posterity the fruits that one should expect from piety, prudence, and good conduct. In the *Aeneid* Virgil has modeled the character of his hero upon the *Odyssey*; he has made him temperate, devout, and hence self-consistent. It is easy to see that Aeneas is not his principal object. In this hero he has seen the Roman people, who owed their descent to Aeneas. He wished to show this people that their origin was divine, that the gods had long prepared for them the dominion over the world; and by this means he wished to get this people to sustain by their virtues the renown of their destiny. Among any of the pagans it is impossible to find a more significant morality than this. The one circumstance in which one might be suspicious of Virgil is that he was in his verses a little too much preoccupied with his own fortune, and that he devoted his poem to the aim of complimenting Augustus and his family in a way that approaches flattery. But I shouldn't want to press my criticism that far.

B. What! You want neither the poet nor the speaker to seek his fortune as a proper end!

A. After our digression upon eulogies, which is not altogether beside the point, we return now to our problem. It involves our knowing whether a speaker ought to be forgetful of self.

B. I don't think he should. You overturn every commonplace truth.

A. Do you not wish that in your republic speakers should be forbidden to speak anything but the truth? Do you not claim that they should always speak to instruct, to reform mankind, and to strengthen the laws?

B. Yes. No doubt of that.

A. Then it is necessary that speakers should fear nothing and should expect nothing from their hearers, so far as their own self-interest is concerned. If you permit speakers to be ambitious and mercenary, will they take sides against all the appetites of man? If they are sick with greed, ambition, indolence, can they cure others of these maladies? If they seek wealth, will it be proper for them to discourage their neighbors from seeking it? I grant that you must not allow the virtuous and unselfish speaker to lack the necessities, but that never happens, if he is a true philosopher, as he ought to be, that is, to reform men's behavior. He will lead a simple, modest, frugal, industrious life; he will need little; that little will not fail to come to him, even if he be obliged to earn it with his own hands; a surplus should not be his reward, and is not worthy to be. The public will be able to do him honor and to give him authority; but if he is free of passion and self-interest, he will use that authority only for the public good, and be ready to lose it whenever it turns out that he can keep it only by dissimulation and by flattering men. Thus the speaker, to be worthy of persuading the people, ought to be an incorruptible man. Without that, his talent and his art become a deadly poison in the republic itself. Hence, it comes about, according to Cicero, that the first and most essential attribute of the speaker is virtue.[14] The speaker must have an incorruptibility that will withstand everything and serve as model for all citizens; without it he will not appear to be convinced of what he says, and as a result he will not be able to persuade others.

B. I concede the importance of what you say. But after all, should a man not be able to use his talents to secure honors for himself?

A. You always go back to the principles. We are agreed that eloquence and the profession of speaker are consecrated to the guidance and the regeneration of the people's morals. In order to do this freely and productively, a man must be forgetful of self. He must teach others the scorn of death,

[14] *De Oratore*, 1.18.83; 2.20.85; 3.14.55.

wealth, pleasures; he must inspire modesty, frugality, un-selfishness, zeal for the public good, an unshakeable devotion to the laws; he must have all this as much in his own conduct as in his speeches. Will a man who seeks to please in order to make his fortune and who as a result has need to humor everybody—will he be able to take hold of the minds of men? Even when he says everything that he ought to say, would they believe what he says when he himself does not appear to believe it?

B. But he doesn't do anything wrong in seeking his fortune, if we grant that he needs to do so.

A. No matter. Let him seek by other means the where-withal he needs for living. There are other professions that can relieve his poverty. If he needs something and is reduced to expecting it from the public, then it is not proper for him to be a speaker. Are you going to choose poor starving men as judges in your republic? Do you not fear that need will reduce them to a certain slack compliance? Would you not rather take men of substance, whom necessity cannot tempt?

B. I would.

A. For the same reason, in getting speakers, that is to say, masters, who are to be obliged to instruct, correct, and mold the people, would you not choose men who need nothing and are forgetful of self? And if there are some who have the talent for these sorts of employment but who yet have interests to conciliate, would you not hesitate to use their eloquence until they had what they needed and would not be further suspected of any self-interest in speaking to men?

B. But it seems to me that the experience of our times demonstrates well enough that a speaker can speak strongly of morality without turning his back on a fortune. Can you behold moralistic portraitures sterner than those now in vogue? People are not offended at all by them—they take pleasure in them. And those who make them do not fail to rise in the world by that road.

A. Moralistic portraitures have no power to convert when they are supported neither by principles nor good practices. Whom do you see converted by that means? You accustom yourself to hear that kind of thing, but it is only a beautiful image that passes before your eyes. You listen to speeches as you read a satire; you regard the speaker as a man who acts well in a kind of comedy; you believe more in what he does than in what he says. He is subjective, ambitious, vain, attracted to a life of ease; he does not give up the things that he says you ought to give up. You let him speak for the ceremony of it; but you believe and act like him. What is worse, you accustom yourself by that means to believe that this kind of gentry does not speak in good faith. That discredits their ministry; and when others speak after them with sincere enthusiasm, you cannot convince yourself that it is real.

B. I grant that your principles are consistent and convincing, when one looks at them attentively; but isn't it out of an undiluted enthusiasm for Christian devotion that you say all these things?

A. It is not necessary to be a Christian to think such things. You must be a Christian to practice them well, because grace alone can check conceit; but it is only necessary to be a rationalist to recognize these truths. Just now I cited Socrates and Plato to you, and you did not wish to defer to their authority; now that reason begins to convince you, and you do not have further need of authority, what would you say if I showed you that this reasoning is theirs?

B. Theirs? Is it possible? I shall be quite relieved to be shown that.

A. Plato has Socrates talk with a speaker named Gorgias and with a disciple of Gorgias named Callicles. This Gorgias was a very celebrated man; Isocrates, of whom we have talked so much, was his disciple. This Gorgias was the first, says Cicero,[15] to pride himself on talking eloquently about everything; in the course of time, Greek orators imitated his vanity. Let us return to the dialogue of Gorgias and Callicles. These two men discoursed elegantly about everything, according to the custom of the former;

15 *De Oratore,* 1.22.103; 3.32.129.

they were fine wits who sparkled in conversation and who
had no occupation except that of talking well; but it appeared that they lacked the thing Socrates sought in men,
that is to say, the true principles of morality and the laws
of an exact and serious logic. After the author has well contrived to make you feel the ludicrous in their character as
wits, he depicts Socrates to you, who, appearing to sport
with them, facetiously reduces the two speakers to the point
where they cannot say what eloquence is. Then Socrates
shows that rhetoric, that is to say, the art of these two speakers, is not a true art; he defines art as "a prescribed discipline which teaches men to do something that is of use in
making them better than they are."[16] By this means he
shows that he recognizes no arts but the liberal arts, and
that even these arts degenerate whenever you direct them
towards an end other than that of guiding men to virtue.
He proves that these speakers do not have this end. He even
makes it evident that Themistocles and Pericles did not
have this end, and hence were not true speakers.[17] He says
that these celebrated men intended only to persuade the
Athenians to make harbors and fortifications and to win
victories. They only made their fellow citizens rich, powerful, warlike, he says; and they were later mistreated for doing so. Thus they got what they deserved. If they had made
their people good by their eloquence, their reward would
have been assured. He who makes men good and virtuous is
sure after his labors to find no ingratitude, since virtue and
ingratitude are incompatible. It is unnecessary to tell you
everything he said about the uselessness of this rhetoric, because all I have said to you about it as if from myself is
taken from him. It would be better to tell you what he says
about the evils which these vain speakers cause in a republic.

B. I well understand that these speakers were feared in
the Greek republics, where they were able to seduce the
people and to make themselves dictators.

---

[16] *Gorgias,* 464, 502-3.   [17] *Gorgias,* 515-19.

A. In effect it is chiefly of this danger that Socrates speaks; but the principles which he gives on that occasion extend farther. In sum, when you and I speak now of a republic to be supervised, we mean not only the states where the people govern, but any state, whether popular, or ruled by several heads, or monarchial. Hence I do not lay stress upon the form of government; in any country the rules of Socrates can be applied.

B. Then explain them, please.

A. He says that, man being made of body and of soul, it is necessary to cultivate the one and the other. There are two arts for the soul, and two for the body.[18] The two arts of the soul are those of legislation and of jurisprudence. Under the art of legislation he includes all the principles of philosophy for regulating the feelings and behavior of particular individuals and of the entire republic. Jurisprudence is the remedy one uses to curb bad faith and injustice among the citizenry; by means of it one decides trials and punishes crimes. Hence, the art of legislation serves to prevent evil, and jurisprudence serves to correct it. There are two analogous arts for the body: gymnastics, which provides exercise, makes the body sound, well-proportioned, agile, energetic, full of strength and grace (you know, sir, that the ancients made an unbelievable use of this art, and we have lost it); then medicine, which cures the body when its health fails. Gymnastics is for the body what the art of legislation is for the soul; it forms, it perfects. Medicine is likewise for the body what jurisprudence is for the soul; it corrects, it cures. But such a state of things, Socrates observes, was changed, pure though it was. In the place of the art of legislation they put the vain subtleties of the Sophists—false philosophers who misuse reason and, wanting the true principles of public welfare, seek their own special ends. For jurisprudence, he continues, was substituted the pomp of the rhetoricians, the gentry who wish to delight and dazzle. In place of jurisprudence, which ought to be medicine for the soul and to be used only to

18 *Gorgias,* 464-65.

cure men's passions, you see false speakers who dream exclusively of their reputation. For gymnastics, he adds, they substituted the art of painting the body and giving it a false and deceitful charm; in place of which you ought to seek only a simple and natural beauty, which comes from health and the proportion of parts, and is neither acquired nor maintained but by system and exercise. For medicine they also substituted the devising of delicious foods and all the stews that tease men's appetites; and in place of purging men who are full of humors in order that their health, and with their health, their appetite, may be restored, they countermand nature and give man an artificial appetite by every contrivance that defies temperance. It is thus that Socrates noticed the disorders in the morals of his time; and he concluded by saying that speakers who, with an eye to curing men, ought to tell them, and tell them with authority, various disagreeable truths and thus give them bitter medicine, instead have ministered to the soul as cooks do to the body. Their rhetoric was merely an art of making stews to soothe sick men; it took the trouble only to please, only to excite curiosity and admiration; speakers never spoke except for such ends as these. He ended by asking the whereabouts of the citizens whom the rhetoricians had cured of their evil dispositions, the whereabouts of the people whom they had made temperate and virtuous. Don't you fancy that you are listening to a man of our time who sees what is transpiring now and speaks of present evils? After having heard this pagan, what would you say of that eloquence which acts only to please and to make beautiful pictures, when it ought, as he said it himself, to burn, to cut to the quick, and to try earnestly to effect cures by the bitterness of remedies and the severity of the regimen? But judge of these things for yourself. Would you find it good for a physician who was treating you to amuse himself, in the extremity of your illness, by spouting elegant phrases and subtle utterances? What would you think of a lawyer who, pleading a case that concerned all the worldly goods of your family, or your own life, indulged in wit and filled his speech with flowers and ornaments, instead of arguing forcefully and arousing the sympathy of the jury? The love of property and of life rather exposes the ridiculousness of such things; but the indifference we have for good morals and religion obscures this ridiculousness in speakers, who ought to be the critics and the physicians of the people. What we have seen of Socrates' attitude towards this ought to make us ashamed.

B. Now I recognize clearly that, according to your principles, speakers ought to be defenders of the laws and masters to teach people virtue; but the oratory of the bar did not go that far among the Romans.

A. That was unquestionably its aim, sir: the speakers strove to protect the innocence and the rights of individuals when they did not have occasion to represent in their speeches the general needs of the republic. Thus it happens that this profession was so honored, and that Cicero gives us so lofty a conception of the true speaker.

B. Let us then see in what way these speakers should speak. I beg you to explain to me your views on this matter.

A. I shall not give you my own views. I shall continue to speak to you about the rules given us by the ancients. I shall moreover give you nothing but the principal matters, because you do not expect me to explain to you in order the almost infinite details of the precepts of rhetoric. Many of them are useless. You have read them in the books, where they are in great plenty. Let us content ourselves with speaking of what is most important. In the dialogue where he makes Socrates speak with Phaedrus,[19] Plato shows that the great defect of the rhetoricians is that they strive for the art of persuasion before they understand, by the principles of philosophy, what are the things which they ought to seek to convince men of. He would have the speaker commence with the study of man in general; and afterwards apply himself to knowing the particular men to whom he will have to speak. Thus the speaker will be obliged to know what man is, what is his destiny, what are his true interests; of what he is made, that is to say, body and soul; what is the

[19] *Phaedrus,* 259-71.

82

true way to make him happy; what are his passions, what
excesses they may have, how they may be regulated, how
they may be usefully aroused in order to make him love the
good; what regulations are fitted to make him live in peace
and to keep society together. After this general study comes
the particular. The speaker must understand the laws and
customs of his country, the connection they have with the
temperament of the people, the manners of each class, their
different degrees of education, the prejudices and interests
dominant in his own time, the means of instructing and reforming the mind. You see that such knowledge as this
amounts to a thorough acquaintance with philosophy. Thus
does Plato show that the role of true orator belongs only
to the philosopher. It is with this in mind that we must
interpret everything he says in the *Gorgias* against the rhetoricians; that is to say, against the kind of person who devises his own art of speech and persuasion, without putting
himself to any trouble to know in terms of principles what
one ought to seek to convince men of. Hence, according to
Plato, the true art can be reduced in essence to a complete
knowledge of what men must be persuaded to do, and to a
thorough understanding of their passions and of the way
to move them in order to achieve persuasion. Cicero has
virtually said the same things.[20] He appears at first to wish
the speaker to be ignorant of nothing, because speakers may
have need to speak of everything and can never speak well
(he observes as Socrates had) except upon that which they
thoroughly know. But then, with an eye to urgent needs
and the shortness of life, he requires the speaker to have
only the most necessary knowledge. At the very least he
would have a speaker well acquainted with all that branch
of philosophy which concerns morals, and would allow him
only to be ignorant of the more abstruse parts of astronomy
and mathematics.[21] Above all he would have a speaker know
the structure of man and the nature of his passions, because
the aim of eloquence is to move the passions according to

[20] *De Oratore*, 1.5.17-18; 1.6.20-21; 1.13.59; 3.14.54-55.
[21] *De Oratore*, 1.15.68-69; *Orator*, 4.14-16.

their inner forces.[22] As for the knowledge of law, he demands that of the speaker, as the foundation of every one of his speeches; but he does not require a speaker to pass his life in plumbing the depths of all legal questions for the small points of trials, because the speaker in case of need can go to legal scholars for what he himself lacks.[23] Like Plato, he requires the speaker to be a good dialectician that he may know how to define, to prove, to disentangle the subtlest fallacies.[24] He affirms that to separate rhetoric from philosophy is to destroy it, and to make orators into childish, superficial declaimers.[25] Not only does he require exact knowledge of all the principles of morality, but also a particular study of antiquity.[26] He recommends the reading of the ancient Greeks; he requires the speaker to study the historians, not alone for their style but also for the facts of history; above all he stresses the study of the poets because of the major connection there is between the images of poetry and those of eloquence.[27] In a word, he often repeats that the speaker must be full of the meaning of things before he speaks. I believe I recall his very own terms, so often have I read them, and so great is the impression they have made upon me. You would be surprised at everything he requires. The speaker, he says,[28] ought to have the subtlety of dialecticians, the knowledge of the philosopher, something close to the diction of poets, the voice and gestures of the finest actors. Notice how much preparation is required for all that.

C. Actually I have noticed on enough occasions that what certain otherwise talented speakers lack most is depth of knowledge. Their minds seem empty. You see that they have been put to no end of trouble to find the wherewithal to piece out their speeches. It even seems that they are not

22 *De Oratore*, 1.5.17; 1.14.60; 2.44.185-216.
23 *De Oratore*, 1.36.167ff.; 1.44.197; 1.15.65; *Orator*, 34.120.
24 *Orator*, 32.113-117; also 4.16.
25 *De Oratore*, 1.5.17; 1.6.20; 3.15.56-74; 3.35.142-43. Also *Orator*, 4.14-19.
26 *Orator*, 34.120; *De Oratore*, 1.5.18.
27 *De Oratore*, 1.34.154-59; 1.16.70; 3.10.39.
28 *De Oratore*, 1.28.128.

speaking because they are overflowing with truths, but that they are seeking for truths because they are overflowing with a desire to speak.

A. Cicero calls them the kind who live from day to day with no provisions; despite all their efforts, their speeches always seem thin and undernourished. There is not time to give yourself three months of preparation before making a public speech; these immediate preparations, however laborious they may be, are necessarily very incomplete, and the capable man demonstrates this as often as the weakling. You must spend many years in getting abundant resources. After this sort of general preparation, immediate preparations cost little. But if you have only applied yourself to the preparation of particular subjects, you are reduced to paying off in the currency of aphorisms and antitheses; you treat only the commonplaces; you utter nothing but incoherencies; you sew up rags not made for each other; you do not show the real principles of things; you are restricted to superficial and often false arguments; you are incapable of showing the full extent of truth, because all general truths have necessary interconnections, and it is obligatory to know almost all of them in order to handle adequately a particular one.

C. Still, most men who speak in public acquire a considerable reputation without other resources than the particular ones.

A. It is true that they are applauded by women and by the vulgar, who let themselves be easily dazzled; but such celebrity never goes farther than a kind of capricious vogue, and even that has to be supported by some clique. People who know the rules and understand the goal of eloquence have nothing but disgust and misgivings for these empty speeches, and are considerably bored by them.

C. You would have a man wait a long time before he speaks in public. His youth would have passed before he had acquired the resources you require of him, and he would no longer be at an age to use them.

A. I would have him put them to early use, for I do

85

not overlook the power of practice; but I would not have him under the pretext of getting practice throw himself at once into outside employments which take away the freedom to study. A young man ought from time to time to test himself; but the study of good books should long continue to be his principal occupation.

C. I believe what you say. All this puts me in mind of a preacher, a friend of mine, who lives, as you have it, from day to day. He does not ponder anything until he is scheduled to preach upon it. Then he closes himself in his study, thumbs his concordance, his Combéfis, his *Polyanthea*, some sermon books he has bought, and various collections he has made of purple patches wrested from their context and hit upon by good luck.[29]

A. You well understand that all that cannot produce a

[29] These are types of reference works used by preachers of Fénelon's time. "Combéfis" refers to François Combéfis (1605-1679), who published many of the works of the Greek Fathers. His most considerable publication, *Bibliotheca patrum concionatoria*, that is, *The Preacher's Library of the Fathers*, which appeared in 8 volumes at Paris in 1662, is the work to which Fénelon here alludes. The *Polyanthea* was as well-known in the seventeenth century as John Bartlett's *Familiar Quotations* is today. In its *editio princeps* it was the work of Dominicus Nanus Mirabellius, often called Nannus or Nani. Its material is alphabetically arranged in the form of expository paragraphs upon a great number of words and phrases, such as *Amor dei, Amor patriae, Amor proximi, Amor sui, Bellum, Dialectica, Fortuna, Futurum, Poeta, Resurrectio, Sacramentum, Trinitas*, etc., etc., each one of which is defined and illustrated from ancient Greek and Roman literature, from the Scriptures, from the Fathers, and from vernacular and Latin secular authors of the postclassical era. All together, Nanus drew upon 173 such sources for his quotations. His collection was first published at Savona in 1503. There were at least five subsequent editions in the course of the sixteenth century: at Venice (1507); at Basel (1512); at Lyons (1513); at Savona in expanded form (1514); and at Solingen (1539). It was later published at Lyons in 1600 and at St.-Gervais in 1604, having acquired somewhere in its several previous editions two new editors, Bartholomaeus Amantius and Franciscus Tortius, whose names now accompanied that of Nanus on the title-page. Their work was re-edited by Josephus Langius at Lyons in 1604 and at Frankfurt-am-Main in 1607 and 1612. New life was again given the work, this time by Franciscus Sylvius, who put out an edition at Lyons in 1620; and it was this issue, bearing the names and the ideas of all five editors, that was kept in constant circulation during the rest of the century by printings at Lyons in 1625, at Frankfurt-am-Main in 1628, and at Lyons in 1648, 1659, and 1669. Doubtless one of these later editions was in Fénelon's mind as he wrote the *Dialogues*.

truly able man. In a case like his, one cannot say anything strongly, one is certain of nothing; everything has a borrowed and patchwork look, nothing comes from origins. One does himself a great wrong to have so much impatience to put himself forward.

B. Then tell us, before you leave, what in your opinion is the major effect of eloquence.

A. Plato says that a speech is eloquent only so far as it acts on the soul of a listener. By that criterion you can with certainty judge all speeches you hear. Any speech which leaves you cold, which only acts to amuse you, and which does not affect your feelings, your heart, is not eloquent, however beautiful it may seem. Do you wish to hear Cicero speak with the voice of Plato upon this matter? He will tell you that the basic effect of utterance must only be its tendency towards the moving of the hidden energies which nature has put into men's hearts.[30] Hence, consult yourself if you would know whether the speakers you hear are doing well. If they make a living impression upon you, if they render your mind attentive and sensitive to the things they say, if they warm you and raise you above yourself, then you may believe without fear that they have reached the goal of eloquence.[31] If instead of moving you or inspiring strong feelings in you, they only act to please you and to make you admire the brilliance and the nicety of their thoughts and expressions, tell yourself that they are false speakers.

B. Wait a moment, if you please. Let me ask you some more questions.

A. I wish I were able to tarry, for I find it good to be here. But I have a matter which I can't postpone. I'll see you again tomorrow and we'll complete this subject more at leisure.

B. Good-by then, sir, until tomorrow.

[30] *De Oratore,* 1.5.17.
[31] Longinus, *On the Sublime,* Sec. 7.

The Second Dialogue

IN ORDER TO ATTAIN HIS GOAL, THE SPEAKER MUST PROVE, PORTRAY, AND STRIKE. PRINCIPLES OF THE ART OF ORATORY, OF THE METHOD OF LEARNING AND DELIVERING SERMONS BY HEART, OF THE METHOD OF DIVIDING AND SUBDIVIDING. THE SPEAKER SHOULD COMPLETELY EXCLUDE FRIVOLOUS ORNAMENTS FROM HIS SPEECHES.

B. It's very good of you to have returned so punctually. Yesterday's discussion has made us impatient to hear the rest of it.

C. As for me, I came in haste, fearing to arrive too late, and not wanting to miss anything.

A. Discussions of this sort are not wasted: you exchange ideas, and you speak on the best things you have read. As for me, gentlemen, I find great profit in discussing things with you—you put up with the liberties I take.

B. Enough of compliments. As for me, I am doing right by myself, and I well know that without you I would still be committed to many errors. Finish ridding me of them, I beg you.

A. Your errors, if you will permit me to say so, are those of the majority of educated men who have not gone deeply into these matters.

B. Then finish curing me. We have a thousand things to say; so let's lose no time—let's come without preamble to the point.

A. What were we speaking of yesterday when we separated? I give you my word, I don't remember.

C. You were speaking of eloquence, and saying that it consists entirely in moving.

B. Yes. But I could hardly understand that. What do you mean by it?

A. Simply this. What would you say of a man who persuaded you without proof? Such a one would not be a true orator. He might be able to seduce other men if he has the

contrivances to persuade them without demonstrating that
what he is inducing them to accept is the truth. A man like
that would be dangerous in the republic, as we have understood from the arguments of Socrates.

B. I agree to that.

A. But what would you say of a man who establishes
truth in an exact, dry, naked way, who puts his arguments
in good order or makes use of the method of geometers in
his speeches, but who does not add anything living, anything figurative? Would he be an orator?

B. No. He would merely be a philosopher.

A. Then, in order to make an orator, we must choose a
philosopher, that is, a man who knows how to establish the
truth; and we must add to the exactitude of his arguments
the beauty and vehemence of a living discourse if we would
make an orator of him.

B. Yes, unquestionably.

A. And it is in this that the difference between the conviction of philosophy and the persuasion of eloquence
consists.

B. How's that? I did not altogether understand.

A. I say that the philosopher acts only to convince, and
that the orator, besides convincing, persuades.

B. I still don't altogether understand. What remains to
be done when the listener is convinced?

A. That remains to be done which an orator rather than
a metaphysician would do in proving to you the existence
of God. The metaphysician will give you a bare demonstra-
tion that does not go beyond theory; to that the orator will
add everything capable of arousing your sentiments, of
making you love demonstrated truth. This is what is called
persuasion.

B. Now I get your thought.

A. Cicero was right in saying that philosophy and eloquence must never be separated; for the knack of persuading, without knowledge and wisdom, is pernicious; and
wisdom, without the art of persuasion, is not capable of

winning men and putting goodness in their hearts.[32] It is well to observe this in passing, in order to understand how much men of the last century deceived themselves. There were, on the one hand, the literary scholars, who sought only purity of language and works elegantly written. These, with their elegance and erudition, and without a sound basis of principle, were for the most part freethinkers. On the other hand, you found the dry and thorny Scholastics, who set forth the truth in so disagreeable and so insensitive a way that they repelled everybody. Pardon this digression. I return to my point. Over and above simple conviction, persuasion therefore has this: that not only does she reveal the truth, but also she paints it as pleasant, and she moves men in its favor. Hence, in eloquence, everything consists in adding to solid proof the means of interesting the listener, and of using his passions for the purpose which one has in mind. One inspires him to anger at ingratitude, to horror of cruelty, to pity for misery, to love of virtue, and so on.[33] There you have what Plato calls acting upon the soul of the listener and moving his feelings.[34] Do you understand now?

B. Yes, I get it. And at the same time I see clearly that eloquence is by no means a frivolous contrivance for dazzling men with brilliant discourses—it is a very substantial art and very useful to morality.

A. From such an estimate comes Cicero's remark that he had seen plenty of fluent talkers, that is to say, men who spoke with charm and elegance; but that one almost never sees the true speaker—the man who knows how to enter the hearts of others and to win them over.[35]

B. I am not surprised at that, and I see clearly that there is hardly a person who sets out for that goal. I declare that even Cicero, who laid down that rule, seems often to deviate from it. What do you have to say about all the flowers with

[32] *De Oratore,* 3.15.56-73; 3.35.142-43.
[33] *De Oratore,* 1.12.50-54; 2.82.337.
[34] *Phaedrus,* 261, 271, 277.
[35] *Orator,* 5.18; *De Oratore,* 1.21.94.

which he has adorned his speeches? It appears to me that they please the mind but do not move the heart at all.

A. One must make distinctions, sir. The works of the young Cicero, where he is only concerned with his reputation, often have this fault: that he appears to be more preoccupied with the desire to be admired than with the justice of his cause. Such a thing will always happen when a litigant employs to plead his cause a man whose only concern in the matter is to discharge his professional duties with brilliance. Accordingly we see that the legal speech was often turned by the Romans into ostentatious declamation. But after all one ought to emphasize that there is in even the most florid of these harangues much that is capable of persuading and moving. It is not in this part of his works, however, that you should look at Cicero to know him well. It is rather in the speeches which he made at a more advanced age in an hour of need in the republic. Then his experience in important affairs, his love of liberty, his fear of the misfortunes that menaced him, impelled him to make efforts worthy of the orator. When he acts to revive a dying freedom and to arouse the entire republic against his foeman Antony, you do not see him searching any longer for conceits and antitheses. It is then that he is genuinely eloquent. Everything of that sort is unstudied, as he himself phrases it in the *Orator;*[36] as indeed it has to be at moments when one needs to be vehement. One becomes a man who without any pretense looks only to nature for everything that is capable of seizing, arousing, and transporting men.

C. You have often mentioned to us these conceits. I should really like to know precisely what they are; for I admit to you that in an actual case I have difficulty in separating the conceit from the other ornaments of discourse. It seems to me that the mind has a sort of good conceit of itself in any artful discourse.

A. Pardon me. According to the selfsame Cicero,[37] there

[36] *Orator*, 23.78. See also St. Augustine, *De Doctrina Christiana*, 4.10.24; and Longinus, *On the Sublime*, Sec. 18.
[37] *De Oratore*, 3.31.125.

are some utterances whose force and subject matter produce every single ornament.

C. I don't understand all these artistic terms. Please explain in familiar language what a conceit is, and what a genuine ornament is.

A. Reading and reflection should be able to teach you the explanation. There are a hundred different types of conceit.

C. But still, for heaven's sake, what is their general characteristic? Is it affectation?

A. It is not every sort of affectation. It is the sort one has when he wishes to please and display wit.

C. That is something. But I still want more precise indications to help me discern them.

A. Oh, well. Here's one of them that will perhaps satisfy you. We have already said that eloquence consists not only in proof but also in the ability to arouse the passions. In order to arouse the passions, it is necessary to portray them. Hence, I believe that all eloquence can be reduced to proving, to portraying, and to striking.[38] Every brilliant thought which does not drive towards one of these three things is only a conceit.

C. What do you mean by "portray"? I don't understand your language entirely.

A. To portray is not only to describe things but to represent their surrounding features in so lively and so concrete a way that the listener imagines himself almost seeing

[38] This statement is an adaptation of Cicero's theory of the three means of persuasion. Cicero believes that the task of persuasion consists fundamentally in proving (his terms for this means are *probare* and *docere*), in winning the hearers' favor (his terms for this means are *delectare* and *conciliare*), and in arousing the feelings (his terms for this means are *flectere, vocare animos, movere,* and *permovere*). See *Orator,* 21.69; and *De Oratore,* 2.27.115, 2.28.121, 2.29.128, 2.77.310, 3.6.23, and 3.27.104. Since Cicero's language in the *Orator* suggests that the second means consists in giving pleasure, Fénelon has to reckon with the apparent inconsistency between his second means and that of Cicero. He does so above, pp. 61-73, and below, p. 95. For St. Augustine's discussion of Cicero's three means, see *De Doctrina Christiana,* 4.12.27. Fénelon appears to be interpreting Cicero and St. Augustine as witnesses against the rhetorical theory of Ramus and Talaeus. See above, pp. 7-46.

them.[39] For example, a dispassionate historian who tells of the death of Dido will content himself with saying that she was so overcome with grief after the departure of Aeneas that she could not bear to live; and that she went upstairs in her palace, threw herself upon a pyre, and killed herself. In listening to these words, you take in the happening, but you do not see it. Listen to Virgil, and he will put it before your eyes. Is it not true that, when he assembles all the surrounding features of her despair, when he shows you the savage Dido, the lineaments of death already etched upon her face, when he makes her speak with her eyes upon Aeneas' portrait and upon his sword, your imagination transports you to Carthage, you believe that you see the Trojan fleet receding from the beach and the queen whom nothing can console. You enter into all the feelings which the actual spectators had as they looked. It is no longer Virgil whom you listen to—you are too attentive to the last words of the unhappy Dido to think of him. The poet disappears. You see nothing but that which he makes visible; you hear nothing but those whom he makes speak. There one sees the power of imitation and of portraiture! Hence it comes about that the painter and the poet have so close a connection: the one paints for the eyes, the other for the ears. Both the one and the other assume the duty of carrying objects over into the imagination of men. I have given you an example drawn from a poet, in order to make you better understand the matter; for portraiture is still more lively and stronger among the poets than among the orators. Poetry differs from simple eloquence only in this: that she paints with ecstasy and with bolder strokes. Prose has its paintings, albeit more moderated. Without them one cannot heat the imagination of a listener or arouse his passions. A simple story cannot move. It is necessary not only to acquaint the listeners with the facts, but to make the facts visible to them, and to strike their consciousness by means

[39] Longinus, *On the Sublime*, Sec. 15; Quintilian, *Institutio Oratoria*, 8.3.61-90.

of a perfect representation of the arresting manner in which the facts have come to pass.

C. I have never grasped all that. I see clearly now that what you call portraiture is essential to eloquence. But you would make me believe that there is no eloquence at all without poetry.

A. You can believe it without fear. It is necessary to exclude versification from the whole matter, that is to say, a prearranged number of stressed syllables, in which the poet encloses his thoughts. The ignorant imagine that poetry consists entirely in such things—they believe one can be a poet if he has spoken or written so as to make his words conform to measure. But the opposite is true. Many people make verses without making poetry; and many others are full of poetry without making verses. Let us then leave versification out of the question. In the last analysis, poetry is nothing but a lively fiction which portrays nature. If one does not have this genius to portray, never can one impress things upon the soul of the listener—all is dry, flat, boring. Since the time of the original sin, man has been entirely enmeshed in palpable things. It is his master misfortune that he cannot for long be attentive to that which is abstract. It is necessary to give a physical body to all the instructions which one wishes to inject into his soul. It is necessary to have images to beguile him. Thus it comes about that, soon after the fall of man, poetry and idolatry, always joined together, entirely made up the religion of the ancients. But let us not digress. You well understand that poetry, that is to say, the lively portraiture of things, is as it were the soul of eloquence.

C. But if true orators are poets, it seems to me that poets are also orators, because poetry is by rights persuasive.

A. Unquestionably they both have the same end. The entire difference consists in that which I have set forth to you. Over and above orators, poets have ecstasy, and this makes them still more elevated, more lively, and more daring in their utterances. You well remember what I told you yesterday from Cicero?

C. What! Is it . . . ?

A. That the orator ought almost to have the diction of the poet.[40] That "almost" tells the whole story.

C. I well understand it now. It's all straightened out in my mind. But let us return to what you promised us.

A. You will understand that soon. To what service in a discourse can anything be put which does not minister to one of these three purposes—proof, portraiture, movement?

C. It will serve to please.[41]

A. Let us distinguish, if you will. That which serves to please in order to persuade is good. Solid and well-expounded proofs are unquestionably pleasing; the lively and natural movements of the speaker have much charm; faithful and animated portraitures enchant. Thus the three things which we make essential to eloquence give pleasure; but they are not limited to this effect. It is a question of knowing whether we shall approve of thoughts and expressions which have no purpose but to please, and which cannot in any way have a more substantial purpose. These I call conceits. Of course, you are always to keep well in mind, if you will, that I praise in discourse all the pleasing traits which minister to persuasion; and that I reject only those wherein the author, full of self-admiration, has sought to exhibit himself and to amuse the listeners with his wit, rather than to absorb them utterly in his subject. Therefore, I believe that it is necessary to condemn not only all puns, for they are only insipid and childish, but also all conceits, that is to say, all those things which serve only for sparkle, and which have about them nothing substantial and nothing conducive to persuasion.

C. I willingly agree to that. But wouldn't you by this severity strip from discourse its principal ornaments?

A. Don't you find that Virgil and Homer are rather pleasing writers? Don't you believe that they are the most

---

[40] *De Oratore*, 1.28.128. Cicero's words are: "verba prope poetarum." See above, p. 84, note 28.

[41] For a reference to the sources of this opinion, see above, p. 92, note 38. For an analysis of the opinion itself, see above, pp. 61-73. See also above, pp. 22-46.

delightful of them all? Yet you will not find in them what are called conceits. Theirs are unpretentious things; nature shows herself throughout; and throughout art carefully conceals herself. You do not find there a single word which appears to be put in to plume up the poet's wit. He stakes his reputation upon not appearing at all, in order to engage you in the things which he paints, as a painter aspires to put before your eyes forests, mountains, rivers, distances, buildings, men, their adventures, their actions, their various passions, without your being able to take notice of the strokes of his brush. Art is clumsy and contemptible whenever it makes itself visible. Plato, who had examined all such things much better than most orators do, assures us that in writing one is obliged always to conceal himself, to make himself forgotten, and to reveal only the things and the persons whom he wishes to set before the reader's eyes.[42] You see how those ancients had standards higher and more substantial than ours.

B. You have told us enough about portraiture. Tell us something about movements. What purpose do they serve?

A. To impress upon the mind of the listener whatever may suit the design of him who speaks.

B. But in what do you make these movements consist?

A. In the words, and in the actions of the body.

B. What movement can there be in words?

A. You will see. Cicero reports[43] that even the enemies of Gracchus were not able to restrain their tears when Gracchus uttered these words: "Wretched! Where shall I go? What sanctuary remains to me? The Capitol? It is inundated with the blood of my brother. My home? I shall see there my unhappy mother dissolved in tears and dying of grief." There you have movements. If you put that into passive language, it would lose its force.

B. Do you think so?

A. You will think so as well as I, if you try it. Look. "I do not know where to go in my grief. No sanctuary remains

42 *Republic*, 393. See also Longinus, *On the Sublime*, Secs. 17, 22.
43 *De Oratore*, 3.56.214.

for me. The Capitol is the place where they have shed the blood of my brother. My home is the place where I shall see my mother weeping in sadness." This is the same thing. What has happened to its liveliness? Where are those broken sentences which so well mark nature in the transports of grief?[44] The manner of saying things makes visible the manner in which one feels them, and it is this which strikes the listeners the more. In such passages as these, not only are sentences completely unnecessary, but one must neglect their order and their interconnections. Otherwise their passion is no longer like real passion; and nothing is so shocking as passion expressed with pomp and in measured periods. I send you to Longinus on this matter; there you will see some marvelous examples from Demosthenes.[45]

B. I understand all that. But you have led us to hope for an explanation of the action of the body, and I am not going to release you from it.

A. I do not pretend to construct on this occasion a complete rhetoric. I am not even capable of doing so. I shall only tell you of some observations which I have made. The action of the Greeks and the Romans was much more violent than ours. We see this in Cicero and in Quintilian.[46] The ancients stamped their feet; they even struck their foreheads.[47] Cicero tells us of an orator who cast himself upon the litigant whom he was defending and ripped his clothes to show the judges the scars he had received in the service of the republic.[48] There you have vehement action; but such a thing was reserved for the extraordinary situation. He does not make mention of continuous gesture. In effect, it is not natural to be forever moving the arms in speaking. It is necessary to move the arms when one is really

[44] Longinus, *On the Sublime*, Secs. 18, 19, 20.

[45] Longinus, *On the Sublime*, Secs. 16, 18, 20, 27, 32, 39.

[46] For Cicero's theory of delivery, see *De Oratore*, 3.56.213-28, and *Orator*, 17.55-60; for Quintilian's, see *Institutio Oratoria*, 11.3.1-184.

[47] *De Oratore*, 3.59.220. See also *Institutio Oratoria*, 11.3.123,128; and Cicero, *Brutus*, 80.278.

[48] *De Oratore*, 2.47.195-96. The speaker in question was Antonius; the client, Aquilius.

97

excited; but it should not be necessary to move the arms in order to put on the outward show of excitement. There are some things indeed which would have to be spoken quietly without stirring.

B. What! Do you mean that a preacher, for example, should not make gestures on some occasions? That would seem very strange.

A. I grant that it has been made the rule or at least the custom for a preacher to strive almost indiscriminately to whip himself up towards everything that he says. But it's rather easy to show that often our preachers whip themselves up too much, and also that they often don't whip themselves up enough.

B. Ha! I wish you would explain that to me, for I have always believed, from the example of * * * ,[49] that there are

[49] This preacher was undoubtedly a contemporary of Fénelon; yet there appears to be no satisfactory way to identify him. Nor is it possible to identify beyond question the various other contemporary preachers whom Fénelon may have made the target of criticism in these *Dialogues*. It should be remarked, however, that there are at least eight preachers designated in Fénelon's analysis of the pulpit oratory of his day, and that the chief opinions as to their identity are inconclusive.

The first preacher mentioned in the *Dialogues* is he who delivered the Ash Wednesday sermon. (See above, pp. 57-61.) The next in order is the minister of *A's* parish, who receives no attention beyond a brief, friendly reference. (See above, p. 57.) The third is *C's* friend, whom we remember as the preacher addicted to the use of sermon aids. (See above, p. 86.) The one to whom *B* alludes immediately above is the fourth. The next is the preacher during whose sermon *A* fell asleep one day. (See below, p. 101.) The sixth is the preacher to whom the pulpit owed much, despite his monotony of voice, his rapidity of speech, his uniformity of action, his lack of genuine fervor, his emphasis upon logic at the expense of striking language, his tendency to memorize his sermons and to speak with his eyes closed. (See below, pp. 102-105, 134.) The seventh is the preacher given to flowery and effeminate eloquence and called by *B* "the Isocrates of our time." (See below, p. 115.) The last, mentioned only in passing, is the one who delivered a constructive but obscure sermon on the morning of the day when the third dialogue took place. (See below, p. 121.)

The first and sixth preacher in this list have received the lion's share of attention from students interested in Fénelon's historical allusions. Stevenson, first to translate the present work into English, suggests that *A's* criticism of the Ash Wednesday sermon, and indeed the other unfavorable allusions to contemporary preaching, are aimed at Esprit Fléchier (1632-1710). (See W. Stevenson, *Dialogues concerning Eloquence*, London, only two or three sorts of movements of the hands to be made in an entire sermon.

A. Let us come to the principle. For what purpose does the action of the body serve? Does it not serve to express the sentiments and the passions which occupy the soul?[50]

B. I believe that.

A. The movement of the body is then a painting of the thoughts of the soul.

B. Yes.

A. And that painting ought to be a genuine likeness. It is necessary that everything in it represent vividly and naturally the sentiments of him who is speaking and the nature of the things he speaks of. I mean that he must not, of course, go to the point where his representation becomes trivial and ludicrous.

1722, p. 4.) Although Fléchier, bishop of Nîmes, was a fashionable preacher of the time when Fénelon wrote the *Dialogues*, and employed a more formal and more elaborate style than that advocated by Fénelon, there is no evidence adduced by Stevenson to prove that it was he whom Fénelon had particularly in mind. J. Lemaitre, *Fénelon*, Paris, 1910, pp. 26-28, says that the criticism of the Ash Wednesday sermon leads us to think of Bourdaloue or Fléchier or Massillon, whereas the reference to the man who spoke with his eyes closed is aimed at Bourdaloue. That Fénelon had Massillon (1663-1742) in mind is hard to believe, unless we accept Lemaitre's statement that Fénelon composed the present work in installments, the first of which was completed around 1690, and the others, much later. The more probable date of the *Dialogues* is 1679, the sixteenth year of Massillon's life, when he would not have been old enough to have invited Fénelon's attack. It is equally hard to believe that Fénelon had Bourdaloue in mind in the criticism of the Ash Wednesday sermon if, as Lemaitre says, Bourdaloue was the preacher accused of speaking with his eyes closed. The latter is treated with respect by Fénelon; the former is not. Thus we must infer that the two references are not to the same person.

A lively controversy has raged over the identity of this preacher who spoke with his eyes closed. Many students have said, as Lemaitre does, that Fénelon meant the reference to apply to Bourdaloue. Others, for the most part biographers and partisans of Bourdaloue, have said that it was Fénelon's intention in the *Dialogues* to create semi-fictional portraits of preachers of the day, not to describe actual contemporaries. But the question remains unsettled. For a dispassionate discussion of it, see E. Griselle, *Bourdaloue histoire critique de sa prédication*, 2 vols., Paris, 1901, vol. 2, pp. 738-64. See also M. l'Abbé Coubé, "Bourdaloue Orateur," *Revue Bourdaloue*, 3 (July 1, 1904) pp. 398-437.

50 Cicero, *De Oratore*, 3.59.221, and *Orator*, 17.55.

B. It seems to me that you're right, and I think I see where you're headed. Permit me to interrupt you in order to show you how I accept all the inferences to be drawn from your principles. You want the orator to express by lively and natural action what his words by themselves could only express in a passive way. Thus, according to you, action itself is a painting.

A. To be sure. But here is what we must conclude from it. It is this: that to paint well, one must imitate nature and see what she does when one lets her act in her own way and when art does not constrain her.

B. I agree to that.

A. Let us see, then. Do you naturally make many gestures when you say unpretentious things in which no passion is involved?

B. No.

A. It would then be necessary either not to make them at all under similar circumstances in a public speech, or to make very few of them; for everything the speaker does ought to follow nature. Furthermore, there are some things upon which one will better express his thoughts by the cessation of all movement. A man filled with powerful feeling stands motionless a moment. This sort of paralysis holds in suspense the mind of every listener.

B. I understand that such pauses when well used are becoming, and are effective in their impact upon the listener. But it seems to me that you reduce the public speaker to doing in respect to gesture only what a private conversationalist would do.

A. Pardon me. The sight of a large audience and the importance of the subject which he is handling ought surely to stir a man much more than if he were engaged in an ordinary conversation. But in public as in private he must always act naturally. His body must have movement when his words have movement, and his body must stand moveless when his words are calm and simple. Nothing seems to me so shocking and absurd as to see a man whip himself into a fury in order to tell me something dispassionate—

while he is sweating, he freezes my blood. Some time ago I fell asleep during a sermon. You know that drowsiness attends afternoon sermons, and that therefore they only preached in ancient times at the morning Mass after the Gospels. I soon awakened and I noticed that the preacher was lashing himself in an extraordinary way. I thought that this was the very crux of his point.

B. Well, what was it, then?

A. He was only notifying the congregation that he would preach on repentance the next Sunday. That notice delivered with so much violence surprised me and would have made me laugh if respect for the place and the service had not restrained me. Most of these declaimers are towards gesture as they are towards voice: their voice has a continuous monotony, and their gesture a uniformity which is not less boring, nor less remote from nature, nor less contrary to the effect which one would expect action to have.

B. You said that sometimes they do not have enough of it.

A. Must that astonish us? They do not distinguish the things which ought to stir one up. They use themselves up on commonplace things and are forced to deliver themselves feebly of the things which demand vehement action. It must even be acknowledged that our nation is scarcely capable of vehemence—it is too superficial, and it does not see things deeply enough. The Romans and even more so the Greeks were distinguished in this particular. The Orientals, especially the Hebrews, excelled in it. Nothing equals the liveliness and strength not only of the figures which they employed in their discourses, but also of the actions which they used in expressing their feelings, as in putting ashes on their heads, in tearing their garments, and in covering themselves with sackcloth in their grief. I do not speak of the things done by the prophets in figuring forth more vividly the realities which they wished to foretell, because those things were inspired by God; but, apart from divine inspirations, we see that those people understood quite differently from us how to express their grief,

101

their fear, and their other passions. Thence unquestionably came those great displays of eloquence which we do not witness any more.

B. Then you would wish great variety in voice and gesture?

A. It is that which makes action so effective and which led Demosthenes to rank it higher than anything else.[51] The more the action and the voice appear simple and familiar in the places where you are only seeking to instruct, to report, and to suggest, the better do they prepare for surprise and emotion in those places where they are elevated by sudden enthusiasm. It is a kind of music: all its beauty consists in the variety of its tones as they rise or fall according to the things which they have to express.

B. But, if one adheres to you in this respect, even our chief orators are rather far from true art. The preacher whom we heard together a fortnight ago does not follow this rule; he did not even seem to bother about it in the slightest degree. Except for the thirty opening words, he delivered everything in the same tone; and the entire difference between those passages where he wished animation and those where he didn't was that in the former he spoke somewhat more rapidly than usual.

A. Excuse me, sir. His voice has two tones, but they are scarcely in keeping with his words. You are right in saying that he does not adhere at all to these rules; I believe that he hasn't even felt the need of them. His voice is naturally melodious; although very badly managed, it does not fail to please. But you see of course that it does not make any striking impression upon the mind such as it would if it had all the inflections which express feeling. His tones are beautiful bells whose sound is clear, full, sweet, and pleasant; but, after all, bells which carry no meaning, which have no variety, and as a consequence no harmony and no eloquence.

---

[51] Cicero, *De Oratore*, 3.56.213, and *Orator*, 17.56; also Quintilian, *Institutio Oratoria*, 11.3.6.

B. But his rapidity of discourse still has many pleasant features.

A. It unquestionably has. And I agree that in certain lively passages one must speak more rapidly. But to speak with headlong speed and not to be able to hold oneself in is a great fault. There are some things which one must emphasize. In this respect the same thing holds for action and voice as for verse: sometimes a slow and grave measure is required to give structure to things of that character, as sometimes a short and impetuous measure is required to signify what is lively and intense. Always to make use of the same action and the same measure of voice is, as it were, to give the same remedy to all kinds of invalids. But you ought to excuse in this preacher his uniformity of voice and action; for, outside of his having very estimable qualities in other ways, this fault is peculiarly necessary to him. Have we not said that it is necessary for the action of the voice always to keep company with the words? His style is completely uniform—it has no variety whatever: on the one hand, nothing familiar, suggestive, popular; on the other, nothing living, figurative, sublime. His is a steady flow of words which are pressing upon one another; his are exact deductions, well-followed and well-drawn arguments, faithful portraitures. In a word, here is a man who speaks in the right terms, and says highly judicious things. It must even be recalled that the pulpit owes him a great debt of gratitude: he has rid it of its servitude to the declaimers, and he has occupied it with great authority and dignity. He is very capable of convincing, but I scarcely know a preacher who persuades and touches less. If you pay heed to it, he is not even firmly grounded; for, besides his not having the least trace of the suggestive and the familiar in his manner, as we have already remarked elsewhere, he has nothing at all of the affectionate, the vivid. His are the arguments which require great concentration of mind. Almost nothing of all that he has said remains in the heads of those who have listened to him. A speech by him is a torrent which passes all at once, leaving its bed dry. In order to make a durable impression, one must help the mind by touching the passions. Dry facts can hardly succeed by themselves. But what I find least natural in this preacher is that he gives his arms continuous movement, while there is neither movement nor figure in his words. The commonplace action of conversation would be suited to such a style as his; or better, such impetuous action as his would be suited to a style full of sallies and vehemence; but even so, as we have said, he would have to manage his vehemence better and make it less uniform. In sum, he is a great man who is not at all an orator. A small-town evangelist who knows how to frighten and make the tears flow strikes much nearer to the goal of eloquence.

B. But what are the means of knowing in detail the gestures and vocal inflections that conform to nature?

A. I have already mentioned them to you. The entire art of the good orator consists only in observing what nature does when she is not hampered. Do not do what bad speakers do in striving always to declaim and never to talk to their listeners. On the contrary, each one of your listeners must suppose that you are speaking particularly to him. There you have what produces natural, familiar, and suggestive tones. In truth, it is necessary that they be always serious and modest; it is even necessary that they become strong and moving in places where the discourse is heightened and full of warmth. Do not hope to express passion by the single instrumentality of the voice. Plenty of people, in storming and in whipping themselves up, merely paralyze the senses. To succeed in painting the passions, one must study the movements which they produce. For example, observe what the eyes do, what the hands do, what the whole body does, and what its posture is; what the voice does in a man wounded by grief or struck with surprise at the sight of a wondrous thing. There you have nature revealing herself to you. You have only to follow her. If you use art, conceal it so well by imitation that one will take it for nature herself. But, to speak the truth, it is in this regard with orators as with poets who write elegies and other impassioned verses. It is necessary to feel passion in order to paint it well.[52] Art, however great it be, does not speak as does actual passion. Hence, you will always be a very imperfect orator if you are not affected by the feelings which you wish to portray and to inspire in others. And it is not out of spiritual-mindedness that I say this—I only speak as orator.

B. I understand that. But you have spoken to us of the eyes. Do they have their eloquence?

A. Do not doubt that. Cicero and all the other ancients confirm it.[53] Nothing speaks so fully as the face. It expresses everything. But of the whole face, the eyes make the chief effect. A single glance thrown to good purpose will strike to the depths of the heart.

B. You make me remember that the preacher whom we were discussing ordinarily has his eyes closed. When you see him close at hand, that grates upon you.

A. That is because you feel that he lacks one of the things which ought to animate his speech.

B. But why does he do it?

A. He is in a hurry to speak, and he closes his eyes because his memory is working too much.

B. I have of course noticed that it is overburdened. Sometimes he even repeats several words in order to recover the thread of his discourse. These repetitions are disagreeable and bring to mind the schoolboy who doesn't know his lesson. They would wreak havoc upon a preacher of less distinction.

A. This is not the fault of the preacher. It is the fault of the method which he and so many others have followed. As long as one preaches by heart and often, one will fall into that difficulty.

B. How, then? Would you want a man never to preach by heart? Then he would never make a speech of any strength and goodness.

[52] Cicero, *De Oratore*, 2.45.189-90; Quintilian, *Institutio Oratoria*, 11.3.61-64.
[53] *De Oratore*, 3.59.221-23; *Orator*, 18.60; Quintilian, *Institutio Oratoria*, 11.3.75-76.

A. I would not want to hinder preachers from getting by heart certain special discourses. They will have enough time to prepare themselves well for those. Still, they can do without them.

B. How is that? What you say seems incredible.

A. If I am wrong, I am ready to take it back. But let us examine it without prejudice. What is the principal goal of the orator? Have we not seen that it is to persuade? And, in order to persuade, did we not say that he had to strike men by arousing their passions?

B. I agree with that.

A. The liveliest and the most striking manner is then the best.

B. That's true. What do you infer from it?

A. Of two orators, which one can have the liveliest and most striking manner? He who has memorized his speech? Or he who speaks without reciting word by word something he has learned?

B. I maintain that it is he who has memorized his speech.

A. Wait. Let's frame the question properly. I put on the one hand the man who carefully writes out his entire speech and commits it to memory to the last syllable. On the other hand I assume the well-informed man who is filled with his subject and has great facility in speaking (for you don't want untalented men mixed up with such matters)—in short, the man who thinks deeply upon all the principles of the subject that he must handle and upon all their ramifications, who puts them in order in his mind, who devises the strongest utterances to make his subject visible, who arranges all his arguments, who prepares a certain number of striking figures. This man unquestionably knows everything that he must say and the place where he must put each thing. The only thing that remains for him to do is to find ordinary diction to give the necessary body to the speech. Do you believe that such a man would have difficulty in finding that?

106

B. What he finds will not be as exact and as graceful as it would be if he devised it at leisure in his study.

A. I grant that. But according to you yourself he will only lack a few ornaments; and you know what we must think about that lack, according to the principles already laid down. In another respect how much will he not gain in freedom and in strength of action, which is the main thing! Suppose him to be well practiced in writing, as Cicero requires;[54] to have read all the good models; to have a considerable skill, both natural and acquired; to be richly grounded in ideas and learning; to have reflected deeply upon the whole of his subject; to have arranged his knowledge thoroughly in his mind—we must infer that he will speak with strength, with coherence, with fluency. His sentences will not delight the ear quite so much. All the better. He will be a better orator for that. His transitions will not be so subtle. That doesn't matter. Besides his being able to have prepared them without getting them by rote, he will have the additional advantage of sharing such negligences with the most eloquent orators of antiquity, who believed that they must often copy nature in this respect and not show too complete a preparation. What then will he really lack? He will fall into a few little repetitions, but they will not be useless. Not only will the judicious listener take pleasure in recognizing nature at work in them—nature, who often repeats what strikes her particularly in a subject; but also such repetition will mightily reinforce truth. It is the authentic way to teach. At the most, you will find in his speech some inexact construction, some term that is improper or that has been condemned by the Academy, some element of irregularity or if you wish something weak and badly placed, which would have slipped out in the heat of battle. But one would have to have a small mind to hold these to be great errors. One will find some of them in the greatest classics.[55] The most skillful of the ancients ignored them. If we had horizons as wide as theirs, we

[54] *De Oratore*, 1.33.152-53.
[55] Longinus, *On the Sublime*, Sec. 33.

would scarcely be preoccupied with these trifles. Those who take delight in such errors as these are unfit to discern greatness. Pardon my freedom. It's only because I know you to be quite different from them that I speak of them with so little caution.

B. You don't need to mince matters with me. Go as far as you like.

A. Then, sir, consider the advantages of the one who does not memorize his speech. He is self-possessed, he speaks naturally, he does not talk in the manner of the declaimer. Things flow from their source. His utterances (if his native character is richly endowed for eloquence) are lively and full of movement. Even the warmth which possesses him converts itself into terms and figures that he will not be able to prepare in his study.

B. But why? Men are animated in their studies and can compose some lively speeches there.

A. That is true. Yet actual delivery adds to them a still greater liveliness. Moreover, what you find in the heat of battle is concrete and natural in a quite different way. It has a casual air and lacks the artifice of almost all discourses composed in leisure. We must add that the skillful and experienced speaker adjusts subject matter to the effect which he sees it making upon the listener;[56] for he notices very well what enters into the mind and what does not enter, what attracts attention, what touches the heart, what does not do these things. He repeats the same things in another way, he clothes them in more striking images and analogies; or perhaps he goes back to the principles from which are derived the truths that he wishes to persuade men of; or perhaps he seeks to allay the passions which prevent these truths from making an impression. There you have the genuine art of instructing and persuading. Without such means as these, you only make vague and fruitless declamations. You see how far from this goal is the orator who speaks entirely from memory. Visualize to yourself a man who dares only to speak his piece. Everything is necessarily

[56] Cicero, *Orator,* 33.117; 35.122.

imprisoned within his language; and he finds happening to him what Dionysius of Halicarnassus notices as having happened to Isocrates[57]—his discourse reads better than it speaks. Moreover, try as he will, his vocal inflections are uniform and always a little forced. This is not a man who is speaking; this is an orator who recites or declaims. His action is constrained, his staring eyes show that his memory labors, and he is not able to surrender himself to an unusual movement without putting himself in danger of losing the thread of his speech. Seeing the manner so much on display, the listener, far from being seized and transported outside of himself, as he ought to be, looks coolly on at every artifice of the discourse.

B.   But didn't the ancient orators do what you condemn?

A.   I believe they didn't.

B.   What! You believe that Demosthenes and Cicero didn't know by heart those perfected speeches that we have from them?

A.   It is clear that they wrote them out. But we have several reasons for believing that they did not memorize them word by word. Even the speeches of Demosthenes, such as they are on paper, reveal not so much the nicety and the refinement of the writer as the sublimity and vehemence of a great genius accustomed to speak vigorously of public affairs. In Cicero you see in various passages of his orations some things that are necessarily improvised. But let us defer to him on this question.[58] He wishes the orator to have a great memory. He even speaks of memory devices as useful contrivances. But the whole of what he says about this subject does not indicate that the speaker must learn word for word by heart. On the contrary, he appears to limit himself to the wish that the speaker arrange carefully all parts of his speech in his mind and prearrange figures and central terms to be used, reserving to himself the opportu-

---

[57] Dionysius of Halicarnassus, *De Isocrate Iudicium*, 2; in his *De Oratoribus Antiquis Commentarii.*

[58] *De Oratore*, 2.86.351-60; 1.34.157.

nity to throw in on the spur of the moment whatever necessity and the design of things would inspire. It is out of such
considerations, indeed, that he demands so much diligence
and presence of mind on the part of the orator.

B. May I say that all this does not persuade me. I cannot believe that a man speaks as well when he speaks without having prearranged every one of his words.

C. As for me, I understand perfectly what makes you so
incredulous. What you have done is to decide the question
upon the basis of ordinary experience. If the gentry who
get their sermons by heart preached without such preparation, they would obviously preach pretty badly. I do not
wonder at that. They are not given to following nature;
they have only sought to learn to write, and to write with
affectation, at that; never have they aspired to learn to speak
in a lofty, strong, and natural way. Moreover, most of them
do not have enough of fundamental doctrine to have confidence in themselves. The method of learning by heart puts
I don't know how many of these limited and shallow souls
in a position to make a public speech with a certain éclat.
They have only to collect a few quotations and maxims.
However little one may have of genius and schooling, one
can in time give a smooth surface to such subject matter.
But in the last analysis serious thought upon first principles
is obligatory, and a wide knowledge of morals, and the
study of antiquity, and the power to reason and to deliver.
Is it not such things, sir, that you ask of the speaker who
does not learn by heart what he is to say?

A. You have put it very well. I want only to add that
when these qualities are not pronounced in a man, he is
not excluded from making some good speeches, provided
that he has a level head, a reasonable fund of knowledge,
and some facility in speaking. In this category as in the
other, there are various gradations among orators. Still, one
notices that most of the men who do not memorize do not
prepare themselves enough. They ought to study their subjects deeply, rehearse all the moves that are capable of
striking home, and add to all that the sort of arrangement

which can serve better than anything else to recall materials to their minds.

B. You have already mentioned arrangement several times. Do you mean by it anything more than division? Haven't you some peculiar opinion upon this point, also?

A. You are pretty close to making fun of me. But in fact I am just as queer upon this point as upon the others.

B. I believe you say that in all seriousness.

A. Don't doubt it. Since we are on the subject, I am going to show you how far most speakers lack order.

B. Since you love order so much, divisions do not displease you, do they?

A. I am quite far from approving of them.

B. Why, then? Do they not put order into a discourse?

A. Ordinarily they put there the kind of order that is more apparent than real. Moreover, they dry up the discourse and make it rigid. They cut it into two or three parts, and these hinder the speaker's delivery and the effect delivery ought to produce. No longer is there genuine unity—there are two or three distinct discourses unified only by arbitrary interconnection. Day-before-yesterday's sermon, yesterday's sermon, and today's sermon, provided that they be planned consecutively, as in Advent, make as much of a unity and a living whole together as the three points of one of these sermons make when they are put together.

B. But to your way of thinking what is order, then? What confusion there would be in a discourse which was not partitioned at all!

A. Do you think that there may be much more confusion in the speeches of Demosthenes and Cicero than in the sermons of your parish preacher?

B. I don't know. I guess not.

A. Don't fear to commit yourself. The speeches of those great men are not partitioned like the sermons of today. Not only they, but also Isocrates, whom we have spoken of so much, and the other ancient orators as well, did not hold to that rule. The Fathers of the church did not recognize it.

111

Saint Bernard, the last among them, often outlines divisions, but he does not follow them, and he does not partition his sermons. Sermons went on for a long time afterwards without being divided, and dividing them is a rather modern invention which comes to us from scholastic philosophy.[59]

B. I grant that the school is a poor model for eloquence. But what, then, was the form anciently given to a discourse?

A. I am going to tell you. The ancients did not divide a discourse. But they carefully distinguished therein all the things which needed to be distinguished; they assigned each thing to its place; and they carefully considered in what place each thing must be put to make it most likely to have an effect. Sometimes a thing does not stand out at all when it is put first; but it assumes decisive importance when it is put in at another place, where the listener will have been prepared by other materials to feel all its force. Often a word put happily into its rightful place puts truth there too in all its light. Sometimes a truth must be left hidden until the end. It is Cicero who assures us of this. The speaker must have throughout a sequence of proofs. The first must prepare for the second, and the second strengthen the first. He must first display his whole subject in the round, and favorably predispose the listener by a modest and suggestive introduction, by an air of honesty and frankness. Then he lays down his premises. Next he sets forth the facts in a simple, clear, and concrete way, emphasizing the circumstances which he will have to make use of soon after. From premises and from facts he draws his conclusions; and he

---

[59] Fénelon's theory of rhetorical arrangement is, I believe, to be construed, not only as his interpretation of ancient theory, but also as his protest against the rigid doctrine of the Ramists. See above, pp. 39-41. In his *Lettre sur les Occupations de L'Académie Française*, Fénelon makes some observations that clarify and extend what he says here about arrangement. See *Œuvres de Fénelon*, 35 vols., Versailles and Paris, 1820-1830, vol. 21 (1824), pp. 178-80. It should be observed that Bossuet's practice in arranging his sermons is not in accord with what Fénelon says in the *Dialogues*, although in other respects Fénelon's view of preaching agrees with that set forth in Bossuet's *Panégyrique de Saint Paul* (1657). For Cicero's theory of arrangement, see his *De Oratore*, 2.76-85; also his *De Inventione*, 1.15-56.

must arrange the reasoning in such a way that all the proofs
help one another to be easily remembered. He ought to
proceed so that the discourse may always go on growing,
and so that the listener feels more and more the weight of
truth. Then he must march out the lively images and the
movements adapted to arousing passion. Here he must understand the connections which the passions have among
themselves: those which he can most easily arouse at first
and then employ to arouse others; those next which can
produce the greatest effects and with which the discourse
must be brought to an end. It is often in season to make
at the end a summary which concentrates into a few words
all the strength of the speaker and puts before the eyes the
most persuasive things he has said. But in the final analysis,
it is unnecessary to preserve this order scrupulously and
uniformly. Each subject has its exceptions and its proprieties. I should add that even within the requirements of
this arrangement, the speaker can find an almost infinite
variety. The order which I have just described is approximately that advocated by Cicero, and it can neither be applied, as you see, to a speech cut into three parts, nor can
it be adhered to in each particular point. Therefore, sir,
order is necessary, but it must be the kind of order which
will not be promised and revealed as early as the beginning
of the discourse. Cicero says that it is almost always better
to conceal it and to guide the listener by it without letting
him see it. He even states in express terms, for I remember
them, that one ought to conceal the exact number of his
proofs, so that no one may be able to count them, although
they should be distinct in themselves; and that one ought
not to have in the discourse any clearly marked partitioning. But the bad taste of later times has gone so far as not
to understand at all the arrangement of a speech unless he
who devises the arrangement gives notice of it as early as the
beginning and brings himself to a halt at each point.

    C.   But do not these divisions serve to assist the mind
and memory of the listener? It is for information that you
make them.

A. Partitioning assists the speaker's memory. Yet a natural order, without being marked, will do the same thing even better; for the actual connection of things guides the mind. But so far as the divisionings of discourse are concerned, they only help those who have studied and whom school has accustomed to the method. And if the people retain the division better than the rest, it is because the division has been repeated more often. Speaking generally, concrete things with some practical application are what they retain best.

B. The arrangement which you propose is perhaps good for some subjects but does not suit all. One does not always have facts to set forth.

A. When you have none of them at all, you leave them out. But there are few subjects where you have none. One of the beauties of Plato is his putting usually at the beginning of his works in moral philosophy some history and some traditions which are at the basis of all the ensuing dialogue. His method would be even more appropriate to those who preach the doctrine of religion; for everything therein is tradition, everything therein is history, everything therein is antiquity. Most preachers do not teach enough, and argue but feebly, because they fail to go back to the sources.

B. You have now talked to us for a long time. I'm ashamed to hold you longer; but my curiosity has the better of me. Let me ask you some other questions about the laws of discourse.

A. Willingly. I'm not yet tired, and I still have a moment to give to discussion.

B. You would strictly banish all frivolous ornaments from discourse. But tell me by concrete examples how to distinguish them from those which are serious and natural.

A. Do you like flourishes in music? Don't you prefer animated notes which objectify realities and express feelings?

B. Yes indeed. Flourishes serve only to please the ear; they mean nothing; they arouse no feeling. Formerly our

114

music was full of them; and therefore it was very confused and weak. Then musicians began to rediscover ancient music. It is a kind of passionate declamation; it acts powerfully upon the soul.

A. I knew that music, to which you are very sensitive, would serve me in making you understand what concerns eloquence. There must then be a kind of eloquence even in music; and we must cast flourishes from eloquence as from music. Do you not understand now what I call verbal flourishes—appointed conceits which always return like a refrain, appointed murmurings of languid and uniform periods? There you have false eloquence, and it resembles bad music.

B. But still, explain this a little more concretely.

A. The reading of good and bad orators will form your taste more surely than all the rules. Still, it is easy to satisfy you by giving you some examples. I shall not take any from our time, although it is fertile soil for false ornament. In order not to hurt anyone's feelings, let's go back to Isocrates—he's so good an example of the flowery and periodic discourse now fashionable. Have you read his eulogy on Helen, which is so celebrated?

B. Yes, I read it once.

A. How did it seem to you?

B. Admirable! I had never seen so much wit, elegance, smoothness, inventiveness, and delicacy. I swear that Homer, whom I read next, did not seem to have the same traits of spirit. Now that you have shown me the true goal of poets and orators, I clearly see that Homer is far above Isocrates just in proportion as the art of the one is concealed, and that of the other isn't. But still, I was then fascinated by Isocrates, and I would be yet if you hadn't straightened me out. M. * * * is the Isocrates of our time;[60] and I see now that in showing the weakness of that ancient orator, you are putting on trial everyone who prizes flowery and effeminate eloquence.

A. I only speak of Isocrates. At the beginning of his

[60] See above, p. 98, note 49.

115

eulogy he extols the love that Theseus had had for Helen; and he imagines that he will give a lofty idea of that woman by unweaving the heroic qualities of the great man who loved her. As if Theseus, whom antiquity always pictured as weak and fickle in his loves, could not possibly have been susceptible to anything mediocre. Then he comes to the judgment of Paris. Juno, he says, promised him empire over Asia, Minerva, victory in his battles, Venus, the beautiful Helen. Since Paris was not able to make his decision (he goes on) by looking upon the faces of these goddesses in all their brilliance, he could only judge in relation to the value to himself of the three things being offered, and to him Helen was preferable to empire and victory. Then Isocrates praises the judgment of him whose discernment even the goddesses submitted to. "I am struck with wonder," he says in favor still of Paris, "that anyone deems him imprudent in having wished to live with her, when so many of the demigods wished to die for her."

C. I imagine myself hearing the antitheses and conceits of our preachers. There are enough Isocrateses!

A. Behold their master. The rest of his eulogy is full of the same traits. It is based upon the long Trojan war, upon the misfortunes suffered by the Greeks to recover Helen, and upon the praise of a beauty so full of power with men. Nothing there is soberly proved. In it all there is not a single moral truth. He judges the value of things only in terms of the passions of men. But not only are his reasonings feeble; even more is his style rouged and effeminate. I have given you this passage, secular as it is, because it is very celebrated, and because its mischievous style is now widely imitated. The more serious speeches of Isocrates savor greatly of the same effeminacy of style and abound in the same false sparkle.

B. I see that you do not want any of these ingenious turns which are neither serious reasons and conclusions nor natural and effective strokes. The example which you gave of Isocrates, even though it is on a frivolous subject, does

116

not fail to be a good one; for all this tinsel is still less fitting in serious and substantial subjects.

A. But let us return, sir, to Isocrates. Am I wrong now in speaking of him as Aristotle did, according to the story Cicero gives us?

B. What does Cicero say of him?

A. That Aristotle, seeing Isocrates carry eloquence from the sphere of work and use to the sphere of amusement and ostentation, and seeing him thereby attract the largest number of students, applied to him a verse from the *Philoctetes* to call attention to the fact that he was ashamed to keep silent and let such a declaimer speak.[61] But that's enough. I must be going.

B. Don't go yet, sir. You won't allow any antitheses, then?

A. Excuse me. When the things one says are in natural opposition to one another, it is necessary to mark their opposition. Such antitheses are natural and constitute unquestionably a solid beauty; they are then the shortest and simplest way of setting things forth. But to take a roundabout way merely to have a display of words is childish. At first people with bad taste are dazzled by things like that; but before long affectations tire the listener. You know the Gothic architecture of our old churches?

B. Yes, I know it. It's found everywhere.

A. Have you not observed its rose windows, its buttresses, its little ornaments carved and connected without plan, in sum, all the gewgaws which it is full of? There you have in architecture what antitheses and other conceits are in eloquence. Greek architecture is much more simple. It only has majestic and natural ornaments. You see nothing at all in it but grandeur, proportion, order. The architecture called Gothic has come to us from the Arabs. Being full of energy and having neither standards nor culture, they were the sort of people who could not avoid surround-

[61] *De Oratore*, 3.35.141. See also Quintilian, *Institutio Oratoria*, 3.1.14. The *Philoctetes* as cited here is supposed to be one of the lost plays of Euripides.

ing themselves with false niceties. Our bad taste in everything comes from their bad taste. They were sophists in argument, devotees of knicknacks in architecture, and contrivers of conceits in poetry and eloquence. These things are all in the same class.

B. That is most amusing. According to you, a sermon full of antitheses and such like ornaments is fabricated like a church built in the Gothic style.

A. Yes, that's precisely it.

B. One question more, I beg of you, and then I'll let you be.

A. What is it?

B. It seems to me that it is rather difficult to treat small matters in a lofty style; and yet it is necessary to do just that if one wants to be sound, as you require him to be. A word on that, please.

A. As a nation we have so much fear of being inferior that we are usually dry and vague in our utterances. Is it our wish to praise a saint? Well, then, we seek out magnificent phrases; we say that he was admirable, that his virtues were celestial, that he was an angel, not a man. Thus we pass our time in exclamations, without proof and without portraiture. Quite to the contrary, the Greeks made little use of all these general terms which prove nothing; but they dealt much with facts. Xenophon, for example, does not once say in his entire *Cyropaedia* that Cyrus was admirable, but he makes us admire him throughout. We too should praise the saints by showing the specific facts of their feelings and actions. We have false aristocracy in such matters as do some provincials who pride themselves upon their noble air. They dare say nothing that does not appear to them to be exquisite and lofty. They are forever stuffed shirts, and they consider themselves to be too much debased by calling things by their right names. Every kind of thing is present in the subjects which eloquence must handle. Even poetry, which is the sublimest kind of eloquence, succeeds only when it objectifies things with all their surrounding details. Observe Virgil representing the Trojan

118

ships as they leave the beaches of Africa, or as they arrive at the Italian coast. Every detail of it he paints. But it must be granted that the Greeks pushed details still farther and followed nature more concretely. Because of Homer's great detail, many persons if they dared would call him too simple. In a simplicity so original and so far lost to our present taste, that poet shows his great kinship with the Scripture. But in respect to painting things simply, the Scripture surpasses him to the degree in which he has surpassed all other ancient writers. In treating a detail, one must present nothing to the mind of the listener which does not deserve his attention and does not contribute to the idea which one wants to give him. Thus one must be judicious in the choice of circumstances, but one must never fear to say everything that has use. It is a badly conceived gentility to omit useful passages because one does not find them susceptible of ornament, quite apart from the fact that Homer's example teaches us rather well how one can embellish every subject after its own manner. Moreover, it must be recognized that each discourse is bound to have its variations. One must be lofty in lofty things; in little things one must be simple without being low. Sometimes simplicity and exactitude, sometimes sublimity and vehemence, will be in order. A painter who never represents anything but palaces of resplendent architecture will never achieve anything of truth, and will weary us before long. One must follow nature in her changes. After having painted a proud city, one often finds it proper to depict a desert and the huts of shepherds. Most men who wish to make beautiful utterances seek indiscriminately throughout to have pomposity of language. They think they have done everything if they have thrown together a heap of big words and vague thoughts. They aspire only to strew their speech with ornaments, like bad cooks who know nothing about how to put in proper seasoning and who think they have given an exquisite savor to meats by dumping in salt and pepper. True eloquence has nothing of the inflated or the ambitious. She moderates and proportions herself to the subjects which she treats and to the men whom she instructs. She is only mighty and sublime when she must be.

B. That word you spoke about the sacred Scripture gives me a great desire to have you make me see its beauty. May we not see you sometime tomorrow?

A. It will be difficult for me tomorrow. Still, I'll try to come in the evening. Since you wish it, we'll speak then of the word of God; for up to now we have spoken only of the word of man.

C. Good-by, sir. I beg you to keep your promise. If you don't come, we'll go look for you.

The Third Dialogue

IN WHAT TRUE ELOQUENCE CONSISTS. HOW THAT OF THE SACRED WRITINGS IS ADMIRABLE. THE IMPORTANCE AND THE METHOD OF EXPLAINING THE SACRED SCRIPTURE. MEANS OF TRAINING ONESELF FOR PREACHING. WHAT OUGHT TO BE THE USUAL SUBJECTS OF INSTRUCTION. ON THE ELOQUENCE AND THE STYLE OF THE FATHERS. ON EULOGIES.

C. I doubted that you would come, and it just barely happened that I didn't go to M. * * * 's house.

A. I had a matter which detained me; but happily I got rid of it.

B. I'm quite relieved at that, for we have great need to finish the matter in hand.

C. This morning I was at the sermon in ———, and I thought of you. The preacher talked in a constructive way, but I doubt that the people understood very well what he said.

A. That often happens. I knew an intelligent woman who said that preachers speak Latin in French. The most essential trait of a preacher is to be instructive. But he must be well instructed in order to instruct others. On the one hand, he must perfectly understand the full meaning of Scriptural utterances; on the other, he must know precisely the capacity of the souls to which he speaks. These things require a very sound knowledge and a large discernment. Preachers speak every day to the people about the Scripture, the church, the two laws, the sacrifices, Moses, Aaron, Melchizedek, the prophets, the apostles; and they do not put themselves to the trouble to make their hearers understand what all these things mean, and what those persons did. A man will follow many preachers for twenty years without understanding religion as he should.

B. Do you think the people are ignorant of the things you speak of?

C.   I myself do not doubt it. Few people understand them well enough to profit by sermons.

B.   Yes, the common people are ignorant of them.

C.   Well, then, the people—is it not they whom one ought to teach?

A.   Add that most gentlemen are common people in that regard. There are always three-fourths of the congregation who are ignorant of those basic rudiments of religion which the preacher presumes them to know.

B.   But would you want a preacher to proceed to explain the catechism to a fashionable congregation?

A.   I am aware that he must use moderation in such matters. But without offending his listeners he can recall the stories which are the beginning and the embodiment of all things holy. Far from being uncouth, such a quest for origins will give to most discourses the strength and beauty which they otherwise lack. I made such a remark yesterday in passing, particularly in regard to the mysteries. The congregation is neither instructed nor persuaded if one does not go back to origins. For example, how will you make people understand what the church has followed Saint Paul in saying so often, that Jesus Christ is our Passover,[62] if you do not explain what the Passover of the Jews was—if you do not show that it was instituted to be an eternal memorial of their deliverance from Egypt and to symbolize a much more important deliverance that was reserved to the Saviour? This illustrates why I said to you that almost everything is historical in religion. In order that preachers fully understand this truth, it is necessary that they be learned in the Scripture.

B.   Excuse me for interrupting you in regard to the Scripture. You told us yesterday that it is eloquent. I was fascinated to hear you say that, and I should really like you to teach me to recognize its beauties. In what does its eloquence consist? Its Latin seems to me barbarous in many passages; I don't find in it any particular delicacy of phrasing. Where then is that which you admire?

[62] 1 *Corinthians,* 5.7.

A. The Latin is only a literal version, in which are reverently preserved many Hebrew and Greek phrases. Do you scorn Homer because we have translated him into bad French?

B. But the Greek itself (for it is the original language of almost all the New Testament) seems quite bad to me.

A. I agree to that. The apostles, who wrote in Greek, knew that language badly, as did the other Hellenistic Jews of their time. That fact explains what Saint Paul says: " . . . I be rude in speech, yet not in knowledge."[63] It is easy to see that Saint Paul is admitting only that he does not know the Greek language well, although in other respects he is exact in explaining to the Greeks the doctrine of the sacred Scripture.

C. But did not the apostles have the gift of tongues?

A. They unquestionably had, and it even passed over to a large number of untutored believers. But so far as the languages are concerned which they already knew by the usual means, we are inclined to believe that God permitted them to speak as they had done before. Saint Paul, who was from Tarsus, naturally spoke the corrupted Greek of the Hellenistic Jews; we observe that he wrote in that way. Saint Luke appears to have known it a little better.

C. But I have always understood that Saint Paul wanted to say in that passage that he was renouncing eloquence and was going to model himself upon nothing but the simplicity of the evangelical doctrine. Yes surely; and I have heard many good men say that the sacred Scripture is not eloquent. Saint Jerome was punished for being disgusted with its simplicity and for liking Cicero better.[64] Saint Augustine appears from his *Confessions* to have committed the same mistake. Did not God wish to put our faith on trial, not only by the obscurity but still more by the crudity of

[63] 2 *Corinthians*, 11.6.
[64] Jerome, Letter 22 (to Eustochium); see F. A. Wright, *Select Letters of St. Jerome with an English Translation* (The Loeb Classical Library), London, 1933, pp. 52-159, especially pp. 125-29.

style of the Scripture, as he put our faith on trial by the poverty of Jesus Christ?

A. I fear, sir, that you go too far. Whom would you rather believe? The Saint Jerome punished for having followed too much in privacy his bent for the studies of his youth? Or the Saint Jerome perfected in sacred and secular knowledge, who invites Paulinus in a letter to study the sacred Scripture and promises him more beauties in the prophets than he had found in the poets? Did Saint Augustine have more authority in his early youth, when the apparent crudity of style of the Scripture disgusted him, as he himself says, than he had when he was composing his books *Concerning Christian Doctrine?* In these books he often says that Saint Paul had an astonishing eloquence, and that its torrent is capable of making itself felt, so to speak, even to those who are sleeping.[65] He adds that in Saint Paul wisdom did not seek for beauty of speech, but that beauty of speech sought out wisdom. He cites great passages from Paul's Epistles and shows them to have surpassed the best art of secular orators. In this comparison he only makes two allowances: the one, he says, is that secular orators deliberately sought out the ornaments of eloquence, whereas eloquence came naturally to Saint Paul and the other sacred writers; the other is that Saint Augustine testifies that he does not sufficiently understand the fine points of Greek to discover in the sacred Scripture the quantity and cadence of periods that one finds in secular authors. I forgot to tell you that he cites this passage from the prophet Amos: "Woe to them that are at ease in Zion, and trust in the mountain of Samaria." He affirms that in this passage the prophet has surpassed the highest achievements of the pagan orators.[66]

C. But how do you take these words of Saint Paul: "Not with enticing words of man's wisdom"?[67] Is he not saying to the Corinthians that he has not come to declare Jesus

[65] *De Doctrina Christiana,* 4.7.11-12.
[66] *De Doctrina Christiana,* 4.7.16-17; *Amos,* 6.1.
[67] 1 *Corinthians,* 2.4.

Christ to them with excellency of speech and of wisdom; that he is determined not to know anything among them save Jesus Christ, and him crucified; that his preaching was not modeled upon the persuasive discourses of human wisdom, but upon the perceived effects of the spirit and the power of God, so that, he continues, your faith should not stand in the wisdom of men, but in the power of God? Now what do these words mean, sir? How could he find stronger language in which to reject the art of persuasion which you are now constructing? As for myself, I grant that I was enlightened when you condemned all affected ornaments that vanity would put into discourses; but your subsequent words do not support your pious beginning. You go on to make preaching a wholly mundane art and to banish from it apostolic simplicity.

A. You are badly enlightened in regard to my esteem for eloquence. And, as for me, I am greatly enlightened in regard to the warmth with which you take me to task for it. Nevertheless, sir, it won't be useless to straighten this matter out. I know many good men who, like you, believe that eloquent preachers do injury to apostolic simplicity. If we come to a right understanding of each other, we will soon be in agreement. What do you mean by simplicity? What do you mean by eloquence?

C. By simplicity I mean discourse without art and without ostentation. By eloquence I mean, on the contrary, discourse full of art and ornament.

A. When you require a discourse to be simple, do you want it to be without order, without interconnection, without serious and conclusive proofs, without means to instruct the ignorant? Do you want a preacher to have no feeling and to make no attempt to strike the heart?

C. Quite the contrary. I want a discourse that will instruct and move.

A. You want it to be eloquent, then, for we have already seen that eloquence is nothing but the art of instructing and persuading men by moving them.

C. I agree that it is necessary to instruct and to strike.

125

But I would have these things done without art and through apostolic simplicity.

A. Let us see then if art and apostolic simplicity are incompatible. What do you mean by art?

C. I mean fixed rules which the human mind has discovered, and which one follows in a discourse, in order to make it more beautiful and more polished.

A. If you only mean by art a sort of contriving to make a discourse more polished in order to please the listeners, I will not dispute your words, and I'll agree that we must keep such art out of preaching; for vanity like that, as we have seen, is unworthy of eloquence and so much the more unworthy of the apostolic preacher. It was only upon that basis that I argued so much with Mr. *B.* But if you mean by art and by eloquence what all the best of the ancients meant, it will be likewise unnecessary to dispute.

C. What then did they mean?

A. According to them, the art of eloquence is made up of the methods which reflection and experience have evolved to make a discourse such as to establish truth and to arouse a love for it in the hearts of men. And it is these same things that you wish to find in a preacher. Didn't you just now tell me that you want order, a method of instructing, soundness of argument, movements of feeling, that is to say, things which strike and arouse the heart? Eloquence is just that, call it what you like.

C. I now see what you reduce eloquence to. When it has such a serious and sober mien, I find it worthy of the pulpit, and even necessary for fruitful instruction. But how do you take that verse of Saint Paul against eloquence? I have already quoted its very words to you. Aren't they explicit?

A. Allow me to begin by asking you one thing.

C. Willingly.

A. Isn't it true that Saint Paul argues admirably in his Epistles? His arguments against the pagan philosophers and against the Jews, in his Epistle to the Romans—are they not beautiful? What he says about the impotency of the law in making men good—isn't that powerful?

C.   Unquestionably.

A.   What he says in the Epistle to the Hebrews upon the insufficiency of the ancient sacrifices; upon the peace promised by David to the children of God over and above that peace which they had enjoyed in Palestine since the time of Joshua; upon the order of Aaron and of Melchizedek; and upon the spiritual and eternal covenant which must necessarily supplant the worldly covenant that Moses had established for a time;—doesn't what he says upon all these things show subtlety and depth of argument?

C.   I agree.

A.   Then Saint Paul did not wish to exclude from discourse all wisdom and all strength of argument.

C.   That is obvious from his own example.

A.   Why do you believe that he would wish to exclude eloquence from it but not wisdom?

C.   Because he disclaims eloquence in the passage which I am asking you to explain.

A.   Doesn't he also disclaim wisdom? Unquestionably. That passage is still more decisive against wisdom and human reasoning than against eloquence. Nevertheless, he himself does not fail to reason and be eloquent—you admit the one, and Saint Augustine assures you of the other.

C.   You make me fully realize the difficulty, but you don't enlighten me. How do you explain it?

A.   Like this: Saint Paul argued, and Saint Paul persuaded; thus he was basically an excellent philosopher and orator. But his preaching, as he puts it in the passage in question, was founded neither upon human arguments nor human persuasions. His was a ministry whose strength came entirely from on high. The conversion of the whole world, according to the prophecies, was to be the great miracle of Christianity. Such was the kingdom of God which came from heaven and which must subject to the true God all the nations of the world. Jesus Christ crucified, declared unto the people, must draw all to him, but draw them by

127

the unique power of his cross. Philosophers had argued without converting men and without being converted themselves; Jews had been the guardians of a law which showed them their shortcomings without supplying a remedy; everyone on earth was convinced of being disordered and corrupted. Jesus Christ comes with his cross, that is to say, he comes poor, humble, suffering for us, in order to silence our vain and presumptuous reason. He does not reason as do the philosophers; but he makes judgment with authority by means of his miracles and his mercy. He shows that he is preeminent. To confound men's false wisdom he places before them the folly and the shame of his cross, that is to say, the example of his profound humiliations. What the world believes to be folly, what scandalizes it most, is what must lead it back to God.[68] Man has need to be cured of his pride and his passion for material things. God grasps him through these things; he shows him his son crucified. Walking in Christ's steps, his apostles preach him. They have recourse to no human means: neither philosophy, nor eloquence, nor statecraft, nor riches, nor authority. Jealous of his work, God does not wish to owe the success of it to anyone but himself. He chooses what is weak, he rejects what is strong, in order more concretely to show his power. He creates out of nothing to convert the world as he did to fashion it. Thus such work must have such divine character as not to be founded upon anything estimable to the flesh. To rest the preaching of the Gospels upon the assistance of nature, as Saint Paul says,[69] would have been to enfeeble and spurn the miraculous power of the cross. It was necessary that the Gospels, without human preparation, should themselves open the heart, and should teach the world by such a miracle that they came from God. There you have human wisdom confounded and reproved. What must be the inference we draw from this? That the conversion of the peoples and the establishment of the church are not due to reasonings and to the persuasive

[68] 1 *Corinthians*, 1.21-31.   [69] 1 *Corinthians*, 1.17.

words of men. It is not that there was nothing in the way of eloquence and wisdom among most of those who declared Jesus Christ; but that they did not place their trust in such wisdom and eloquence—they did not pursue these things as something that would be required to give authority to their words. Everything, as Saint Paul says, is founded not upon the persuasive discourses of human philosophy, but upon the influences of the spirit and the power of God, that is to say, upon miracles which strike the eyes and upon the interior operation of grace.

C. According to you, then, one spurns the cross of the Saviour if one in preaching supports himself upon human wisdom and eloquence.

A. Yes, unquestionably. The ministry of the word rests wholly upon faith. One must pray, one must purify his heart, one must expect everything to come from on high, one must arm himself with the sword of the word of God and count not at all upon his own word—that is the essential preparation. But although the inward fruit of the Gospels is due only to pure grace and to the power of the word of God, there are still various things which men should do on their side.

C. Up to now you have spoken well; but I see that you are going to return to your first opinions.

A. I don't think I've departed from them. Don't you believe that the work of our salvation depends upon grace?

C. Yes, that is the creed.

A. Nevertheless you remember that prudence is required in choosing reliable courses of life and in avoiding the occasions of danger. Don't you want one to be on his guard as well as to pray? When you are on your guard and pray, will you have spurned the mystery of grace? Unquestionably not. We owe all to God; but God subjects us to an outward order of human contrivances. The apostles did not pursue the vain ostentation and frivolous elegancies of the pagan orators; they did not take kindly to the subtle arguments of the philosophers, who made everything depend upon the very reasonings with which they intoxicated themselves, as Saint Paul puts it; they contented themselves with preaching Jesus Christ with all the strength and all the grandeur of the language of the Scripture. True, they had no need of any preparation for their ministry, because the Holy Spirit, descended upon them to their sight, gave them words on the spur of the moment. The difference then between the apostles and their successors is that their successors, not being miraculously inspired as they were, have need to prepare themselves and to fill themselves with the doctrine and spirit of the Scripture in order to compose their discourses. But such preparation ought never to entice them to speak less simply than did the apostles. Would you not be happy if preachers were not more ornate in their discourses than Saint Peter was, and Saint Paul, and Saint James, and Saint Jude, and Saint John?

C. I agree that I should be. And I grant that since eloquence, as you put it, consists only in the order and the strength of the words by which one persuades and moves, it does not disgust me as much as it did. I have always taken eloquence to be an entirely secular art.

A. Two sorts of persons have the same idea of it: first, the false orators, and we have seen how much they are misled when they seek eloquence as a vain display of words; and secondly, those good men who are not sufficiently instructed, and in their case you see them in humility renouncing eloquence as a display of words, yet pursuing true eloquence whenever they endeavor to persuade and move.

C. Now I understand what you say. But let us return to the eloquence of the Scripture.

A. To sense it you will find nothing more useful than to have a taste for ancient simplicity. The reading of the ancient Greeks best serves to make you generously eloquent. I say the ancient Greeks; for those Greeks whom the Romans scorned with so much reason and called *Graeculi*[70] had wholly degenerated. As I told you yesterday, one must know Homer, Plato, Xenophon and the others of the early ages. After reading them, you will no longer be surprised

70 *De Oratore,* 1.11.47; 1.22.102; 1.51.221.

at the Scripture. Both have almost the same customs, the same stories, the same symbols of great things, the same impulsions. The difference between them is entirely to the credit of the Scripture. It surpasses them infinitely in simplicity, in liveliness, in grandeur. Even Homer never approached the majesty of the hymns of Moses, particularly the last,[71] which all the children of Israel had to learn by heart. Never was any Greek or Latin ode able to achieve the grandeur of the Psalms. For example, that which begins thus, "The mighty God, even the Lord, hath spoken, and called the earth . . . ,"[72] surpasses all human imagination. Neither Homer nor any other poet has ever equaled Isaiah depicting the mightiness of God, in whose eyes the nations are but a grain of dust, the universe but a tent raised up today and taken down tomorrow. At times this prophet has all the sweetness and tenderness of an eclogue in the smiling pictures that he draws of peace; at times he rises and leaves everything below him.[73] But what is there in pagan antiquity to compare with the tender Jeremiah deploring the misfortunes of his people, or with Nahum seeing proud Nineveh far off in his mind's eye laid waste under the blows of an innumerable army? You believe you see that army; you believe you hear the clash of arms and chariots. All is painted in a living style to seize the imagination. He leaves Homer far behind him. Likewise read Daniel proclaiming to Belshazzar the vengeance of God about to engulf him; and look in the loftiest classics of antiquity for anything that one can compare to these passages. Moreover, everything is self-sustained in the Scripture, everything preserves the character that it ought to have—the history, the precise detail of laws, the descriptions, the vehement passages, the mysteries, the moral discourses. In sum, there is as much difference between the secular poets and the prophets as there is between genuine and pretended enthusiasm. The ones, actually inspired, ex-

[71] *Deuteronomy*, 32.
[72] In the Vulgate, *Psalm* 49; in the King James Version, *Psalm* 50.
[73] *Isaiah*, 40.15, 22; 11.6-9; 35.5-10.

press concretely something of the divine; the others, laboring to transcend themselves, always allow human weakness to show in them. Only the second book of Maccabees, the Book of Wisdom particularly at the end, and that of Ecclesiasticus particularly at the beginning, show the bombast of the style which the Greeks, then in a state of decline, had spread throughout the Orient, where their language had been established along with their domination. But it is vain in me to hope to tell you of these things; they must be read to be felt.

B. I am anxious to have a try at it. One ought to devote oneself to such study more than one does.

C. I well imagine that the Old Testament is written with that grandeur and those vivid portraitures that you told us of. But you say nothing about the simplicity of the words of Jesus Christ.

A. His simplicity of style is completely to the ancient taste. It corresponds both to Moses and to the prophets, whose words Jesus Christ borrows quite often. But simple and familiar as it is, it is sublime and symbolic in many places. It will be easy to prove in detail, with the texts in hand, that we have no preacher of our time who has been as figurative in his best-wrought sermons as Christ was in his preaching to the people. I do not speak of his discourses as reported by Saint John, where almost everything is visibly divine. I speak of his plainest discourses as recorded in the other Gospels. The apostles wrote in the same way, with this difference: that Christ, the master of his doctrine, preaches it in full serenity; he says what he pleases, and he says it without any effort; he speaks of the kingdom and the heavenly glory as of his Father's house. Every grandeur that strikes us with astonishment is natural to him. He is born to them, and he speaks what he sees, as he himself assures us.[74] On the other hand, the apostles falter under the weight of the truths revealed to them; they are not able to express all that they see; words fail them. Thereby come their transpositions, their ambiguous utterances, their unfinished

[74] *John,* 8.38.

joints of speech. All such irregularity of style indicates, in Saint Paul and the other apostles, that the spirit of God was hurrying them along; but notwithstanding these small disorders of diction, everything of theirs is noble, lively, and striking. As for the *Apocalypse*, you find the same magnificence and the same enthusiasm in it as in the prophets: terms are often the same, and sometimes this resemblance makes them of service to each other in being understood. Now you see that eloquence does not belong only to the books of the Old Testament, but is also found in the New.

C.   Granting that the Scripture is eloquent, what do you infer?

A.   That those whose duty it is to preach it can without qualms copy or rather borrow its eloquence.

C.   Hence one should choose from it the passages that he finds most beautiful.

A.   It disfigures the Scripture to make it known to Christians only through detached passages. Such passages, beautiful as they are, cannot alone make all their beauty felt, when one does not know their context; for everything is consecutive in the Scripture, and this consecutiveness is its grandest and most astonishing feature. Failing to understand it, one takes these passages in the wrong sense; one makes them say whatever one wishes, and one satisfies himself with ingenious interpretations which, being arbitrary, have no power to persuade men and change their habits.

B.   What then would you demand of these preachers? That they do nothing but follow the text of the Scripture?

A.   Wait. At least I would want preachers not to be satisfied with pasting together similar passages. I would want them to explain the principles and the interconnections of the doctrine of the Scripture. I would want them to capture its spirit, its style, its figures, that all of their discourses might serve to convey the understanding and the flavor of it. They need nothing more to be eloquent; for only to do thus would be to imitate the most perfect model of eloquence.

B. But to achieve this, it would be necessary, then, as I said, to explain the sequence of the text.

A. I would not want to hold all preachers to that. One can preach sermons upon the Scripture without explaining it book after book. But we must admit that preaching would be quite another thing if preachers, following the ancient custom, explained to the people the holy books one after the other. Calculate for yourself what authority a man would have if he said nothing of his own devising and did nothing but follow and explain the thought and the word of God. Moreover, he would be doing two things at once: in explaining the truths of the Scripture, he would be interpreting its text, and would be habituating Christians always to see the relation between the meaning and the letter. What more is needed to accustom them to nourish themselves upon this sacred bread! A congregation which had already heard all the principal points of the ancient law explained would be much more in a condition to profit by the explanation of the new law than are most Christians today. That preacher of whom we were speaking not long ago has this fault among his great virtues: that his sermons are attractive arguments upon religion but are not religion itself. We are too much given to moral portraiture, and we do not explain enough the principles of the evangelical doctrine.

C. That is because it is much easier to paint the disorders of the world than to explain soundly the basis of Christianity. For the former, one needs only to be experienced in the doings of the world and to be able to command language. For the latter, a serious and profound contemplation of the sacred Scripture is required. Few men know religion fully enough to explain it well. Most of them deliver beautiful sermons, but they would not know how to compose a sound catechism, much less a homily.

A. You have hit the nail on the head. Thus most sermons are the reasonings of philosophers. Sometimes we only cite the Scripture as an afterthought for the sake of appearance or ornament. Then it is no longer the word of God; it is the word and the contrivance of men.

C. You agree that such men work to cast out the cross of Christ.

A. I leave them to you. I confine myself to the eloquence of the Scripture, which evangelical preachers ought to copy. Thus we are in agreement, provided that you make no exception for certain zealous preachers who, under a pretext of apostolic simplicity, do not deeply study either the doctrine of the Scripture or the marvelous way God teaches us in it to persuade men. They imagine that they have only to scream and to speak often of the devil and hell. It is unquestionably necessary to strike people with living and terrible images; but it is from the Scripture that one learns how to make these powerful effects. One also learns admirably from it the way to make instructions concrete and popular, without making them lose the weight and power they ought to have. Lacking these insights, the preacher often does no more than daze the people. Distinct truths hardly stay in their minds, and even their awareness of fear is not lasting. The simplicity that he affects is often only an ignorance and vulgarity that try the patience of God. Nothing can excuse such men but the honesty of their intentions. They ought to have studied and contemplated the sacred Scripture for a long time before they preach. A preacher who knows that book well, and who has a talent for speaking, joined to the authority of his ministry and his good example, will not have need of a lengthy preparation in order to make excellent discourses. One speaks easily of things when he fully knows and loves them. A subject like that of religion furnishes high thoughts above all, and arouses the largest feelings. These are the things which produce true eloquence. But we ought to find in a preacher the father who speaks to his children with tenderness, rather than the declaimer who articulates with emphasis. So is it devoutly to be wished that the ministry had had as a general rule only shepherds who gave fodder to the flocks according to their needs. In order to bring this about, pastors should be chosen only from that part of the priesthood which has the gift of speech. A contrary policy brings two evils: the one, that pastors who preach not at all or who speak without skill, are not greatly valued; the other, that the office of volunteer preacher attracts to it I know not how many vain and ambitious spirits. You know that the preaching of the word was reserved to bishops for many centuries, particularly in the West. You remember the case of Saint Augustine, who, against the usual rule, was engaged to preach while yet only a priest, because Valerius, his predecessor, was a foreigner who did not speak fluently. This was the beginning of our custom in the West. In the East they began earlier to make priests preach, the sermons which Saint Chrysostom made at Antioch while only a priest being an indication of it.

C. I share your sentiments in that matter. Only pastors should as a rule be allowed to preach. This would be the way to restore to the pulpit the simplicity and authority that it ought to have; for pastors who had experience in doing work and in guiding souls, and who combined that with a knowledge of Scripture, would speak in a way much more suited to the needs of their hearers; whereas the preachers who only have theoretical knowledge deal much less with their hearers' difficulties, hardly ever adjust themselves to their hearers' state of mind, and speak in the vaguest of terms. These, then, are concrete reasons for preferring the sermons of the pastor to those of other preachers; and there is the further one that the pastor's very voice has a benevolent authority. To what purpose so many young, inexperienced, unlearned, unsaintly preachers? It would be worth far more to have fewer sermons and to have them better.

B. But there are many priests who are not pastors and yet preach with great effect. How many monks there even are who would worthily fill the pulpit!

C. I agree to that. Hence, I would make them be pastors. These are the ones who must in spite of themselves be given the task of caring for souls. Did they not formerly seek among the hermits for those whom they wished to elevate to high office in the church?

A. But it is not for us to prescribe the discipline. Each age has its customs according to its needs. Let us respect, sir, all the forbearances of the church; and without any spirit of criticism, let us finish constructing a true preacher according to our ideal.

C. It seems to me that I can already construct him completely out of the things you have said.

A. Let us see what you think him to be.

C. I would want him to have studied thoroughly during his youth whatever is most useful in Greek and Latin poetry and eloquence.

A. That is not necessary. True, when one has studied such things well, he can draw great benefits from them in respect, even, to understanding the Scripture, as Saint Basil has shown us in his treatise expressly written upon this subject.[75] But after all, one can dispense with them. In the first ages of the church, they effectively dispensed with them. Those who had studied such things when they were worldlings drew some great benefits for religion from them upon becoming pastors later. But these studies were not allowed to those who were ignorant of them during the time when they were engaged in the study of holy writ.[76] The conviction was that the Scripture sufficed. Hence comes what you see in the *Apostolical Constitutions*, where the faithful are urged not to read pagan authors.[77] If you want to know history, says this book, if you want to know law, moral precepts, eloquence, poetry, you find it all in the Scripture. In effect, one does not need, as we have seen, to look elsewhere for what can form taste and judgment, even in respect to

[75] Basil, "Address to Young Men on Reading Greek Literature"; see R. J. Deferrari and M. R. P. McGuire, *Saint Basil The Letters with an English Translation* (The Loeb Classical Library), 4 vols., London, 1926-1934, vol. 4, pp. 378-435.

[76] St. Augustine, *De Doctrina Christiana*, 2.39.58.

[77] *The Apostolical Constitutions*, 1.6; see *Ante-Nicene Christian Library*, ed. by A. Roberts and J. Donaldson, 24 vols., Edinburgh, 1867-1872, vol. 17, part 2, pp. 20-21.

eloquence. Saint Augustine observes that the poorer one is in his own inner self, the more he ought to enrich himself from the sacred sources; and that being by himself small in expressing such great things, he has need to grow by feeding upon the very authority of the Scripture.[78] But pardon me for having interrupted you. Continue, please.

C. Ah, well, we'll content ourselves with the Scripture, then. But shall we not add the Fathers?

A. Unquestionably. They are the canals of transmission; it is through them that we discover the way in which the church has interpreted the Scripture in every century.

C. But must one always undertake to explain all passages according to the interpretations that the Fathers have given them? It seems to me that one of these authorities often gives one figurative meaning to a passage, and another, another. Which one is to be chosen? For you would never have done, if you had to consider them all.

A. When we say that it is always necessary to explain the Scripture according to the doctrine of the Fathers, we mean, according to their constant and uniform doctrine. They have often given godly interpretations which are not at all literal and are not founded upon the doctrine of the mysteries and of the outward signs of the prophets. Such meanings are arbitrary, and one is not obliged to follow them, inasmuch as they do not follow one another. But in those places where the Fathers explain the opinion of the church upon the doctrine of faith, or upon the principles of conduct, it is not permitted to give the Scripture a meaning contrary to their opinion. Here you have the way in which their authority is to be recognized.

C. That seems clear to me. I should want a preacher to know the essence of their doctrine before he begins to preach, so that he will conform to it. I should even want him to study their theories of conduct, their rules concerning moderation, and their method of giving instruction.

[78] *De Doctrina Christiana,* 4.5.8.

A. Excellent. They are our masters. They were lofty minds, great souls full of heroic feeling, men who had a marvelous experience with the attitudes and the conduct of humanity, and who had acquired a great authority and a great skill in speaking. You even find them highly polished, that is, perfectly instructed in all the proprieties, whether of writing, or speaking in public, or conversing familiarly, or fulfilling all the duties of citizenship. Unquestionably all such things acted to make them highly eloquent and completely fitted to win men. Thus we find in their works a refinement not only of utterance but of feeling and character that we do not encounter in the writers of succeeding ages. This refinement, which harmonizes well with simplicity and makes patristic writings so charming and suggestive, produced profound effects upon religion. It is a refinement like theirs that cannot possibly be studied in excess. Thus, along with the Scripture, their works are the uncontaminated sources of good sermons.

C. When a man has acquired this groundwork and when the virtues exemplified by him have satisfied the church, he will be in a position to explain the Gospels with great authority and profit. If he is given simple instructions and made to practice discourses at an early period, he will develop liberty and facility enough to speak well. I repeat again that such men, being occupied with every detail of their ministry—with administering the sacraments, with guiding souls, with consoling the dying and the afflicted—will have no time to write out learned sermons and get them by heart. Instead, their mouths must speak from the abundance of their hearts;[79] that is, they must spread out before the people the fullness of their Gospel knowledge and their own tender feelings. Concerning what you said yesterday of sermons learned by heart, I had the curiosity to go look up a passage of Saint Augustine which I had read one time, and here is the sense of it:[80] he affirms that preachers should speak more clearly and more

[79] *Matthew*, 12.34.
[80] *De Doctrina Christiana*, 4.10.25.

concretely than other men, because, since custom and propriety do not permit them to be interrogated, it is their obligation to fear that they are not adjusting themselves enough to their listeners. That is why, says he, that those who learn their sermons word for word, and who are unable to repeat and clarify a truth to the point where they know it has been understood, deprive themselves of a great advantage. You see by this that Saint Augustine was satisfied with preparing the subject in his mind, and did not commit to memory every word of his sermons. Although the rules of true eloquence will demand something more, those of the ministry of the Gospel do not allow him to go farther. So far as I am concerned, I have been of your opinion upon this matter for a long time. As long as there are so many pressing needs in Christianity, as long as the preacher, whose duty it is to be a man of God and to be fitted for every good work,[81] makes haste to uproot ignorance and offenses from the fields supervised by the church, I believe it is highly unworthy of him to pass his life in his study, rounding out periods, retouching portraitures, and contriving rhetorical divisions; for when you have put yourself into the shoes of that sort of preacher, you have no time to do other things, you do not any longer indulge in other studies or other work, you even are reduced now and then to repeating the same sermons over and over, in order to find time for relaxation. What eloquence has he whose listeners know in advance his every phrase, his every movement! Truly, such are the ways to surprise, to astonish, to mollify, to seize, and to persuade men! There you have a strange way to conceal art and to make nature speak! As for me, all that frankly scandalizes me. What! Shall the dispenser of the mysteries of God be an idle declaimer, jealous of his reputation and a lover of vain ostentation? Shall he not dare speak of God to the people without having ordered all of his words and learned his schoolboy lesson by heart?

A. Your zeal gives me pleasure. What you say is true. Still, you ought not to say it too emphatically; for you must

[81] 2 *Timothy,* 3.17.

140

treat kindly the many men of merit and even righteousness who, out of deference to custom, or concerned with the example they set, are engaged in all honesty with the method which you condemn with good reason. But I am ashamed to interrupt you so often. Finish, I beg of you.

C. I would want a preacher to explain all of religion; and to develop it concretely; and to show how things were established; and to emphasize their sequence and tradition; and, in showing thus the origin and the foundation of religion, to destroy the objections of unbelievers without undertaking to attack them openly, for fear of alienating the faithful.

A. That is well said. For the real way to prove the truth of religion is to explain it well. It proves itself when you give the true idea of it. All other proofs, which are not drawn from the depths and the circumstances of religion itself, are as it were foreigners to it. For example, the best proof of the creation of the world, of the flood, and of the miracles of Moses, is the nature of those miracles and the way in which their history has been written. The wise and dispassionate man needs only to read them to feel their truth.

C. I would also want a preacher to explain diligently and consecutively to the people, not only every detail of the Gospels and the mysteries, but also the origin and the institution of the sacraments, the traditions, disciplines, duty, and ceremonies of the church. These matters fortify the faithful against the objections of heretics and put them in a position to give a reasonable account of their faith and even to sway those of the heretics who are not stubborn. All such teachings will strengthen faith, give a lofty idea of religion, and make the people profit to their own satisfaction by everything they see in the church; whereas, given superficial instruction, they understand almost nothing of what they see, and they have only a very confused idea of what they hear the preacher say. It is principally on account of this sequence of teachings that I would want such men as pastors appointed to preach in each parish. I have often observed that there is no art and no science in the world which masters do not teach in sequence by means of principles and with method. It is only religion which is not taught to the faithful in such a way. We give them a brief dry catechism in their childhood, and make them get it by heart without understanding its meaning. After that they have nothing more for their instruction but vague and unrelated sermons. I would want all Christians, as you put it just now, to be taught the primary elements of their religion and to be led systematically to the highest mysteries.

A. That is what they used to do. They began with the Catechism, after which the pastors taught the Gospels in sequence by means of homilies. This made Christians well schooled in all the word of God. You remember the book of Saint Augustine, *De Catechizandis Rudibus.* You also remember Saint Clement's *Pedagogue,* a work written to make the ethics of Christian philosophy known to the pagans who were being converted. It was the very greatest men who were employed in these teachings. Thus they produced astonishing results, which to us now appear almost unbelievable.

C. Finally, I would have a preacher, whoever he may be, make his sermons in such a way that they will not be a heavy burden to him and that therefore he will be able to preach often. It is necessary that all his sermons be brief, and that he be able, without inconveniencing himself and tiring the people, to preach every Sunday after the Gospel reading. Apparently those former bishops, who were well advanced in years and burdened with so much work, did not make as much of a ceremony as our preachers do of speaking to the people in the middle of the Mass, or of solemnizing the Mass every Sunday themselves. Nowadays, in order for a preacher to do well, he must be sweating, breathless, and incapable of activity for the rest of the day, when he steps down from the pulpit. The chasuble, which did not then have openings at the shoulders as at present, and which hung down equally on all sides, apparently hindered them from moving their arms as much as our preachers do.

Hence, their sermons were short, and their action sober and moderate. Ah, well, sir, is not all this in accord with your principles? Is not this your conception of the sermon as you gave it to us?

A. It is not mine. It is that of antiquity. The more I go into it, the more I find that the ancient formula for sermons was the best. Those were great men; men who were not only of profound holiness but also deeply enlightened about the foundation of religion and about the way to persuade mankind; men who took pains to reduce all these things to rule. Their air of simplicity concealed a marvelous wisdom. You can't imagine being able to find anything better in succeeding ages. You have explained all this perfectly, sir, and have left me nothing to say. You speak my thought better than I do.

B. You put the eloquence and the sermons of the Fathers upon a very high plane.

A. I don't think I exaggerate.

B. I am surprised to notice that, after having been so severe with secular orators who strewed conceits about in their speeches, you are so indulgent towards the Fathers, who themselves are full of conceits, antitheses, and epigrams, in violation of all your rules. For mercy's sake, be consistent, and explain all this. For example, what do you think of Tertullian's style?

A. There are very estimable things in that author. The grandeur of his feeling is often admirable. Besides, he must be read for various principles about tradition, for facts of history, and for the modes of discipline of his time. But for his style, I do not care to defend it. He has many false and obscure sentences, many hard and distorted metaphors. What is bad in him is the very thing that most of his readers seek after most. Many preachers ruin themselves by reading him. Their thirst to say something unusual leads them to study him. His diction, which is extraordinary and full of parade, fascinates them. You must keep well away, then, from imitating his phrases and style; but you can

143

draw great sentiments and an understanding of antiquity from his works.

B. But what think you of Saint Cyprian? Isn't he also rather bombastic?

A. He unquestionably is. One could scarcely be otherwise in his age and country. But although his style and diction betray the bombast of his time and the harshness of Africa, he still has much strength and eloquence. Throughout his works one finds a great spirit, an eloquent soul, who sets forth his sentiments in a lofty and striking way. One finds here and there affected ornaments; for example, in the Epistle to Donatus, which Saint Augustine nevertheless cites as a letter shot through with eloquence.[82] The latter says that God permitted these strokes of affected eloquence to appear in Saint Cyprian, in order to teach posterity how Christian exactitude had purified all the rest of his works of whatever there was of superfluous ornament in his oratorical style, and had confined him to the limits of a soberer and more modest eloquence. It is this latter characteristic, as displayed in all the subsequent letters of Saint Cyprian, continues Saint Augustine, which one can love with confidence and can imitate without violating the rules of the severest religion, but which one can only equal with great difficulty. In the last analysis, Saint Cyprian's Epistle to Donatus, although too ornamented, even in the judgment of Saint Augustine, deserves to be called eloquent; because, although one finds there, as he says, a few too many planted flowers, one sees nevertheless that the main body of the letter is highly serious, very lively, and excellently suited to give a lofty idea of Christianity to a pagan whom one would convert. In those passages where Saint Cyprian is deeply aroused, he leaves behind all conceits and falls into a style both vehement and sublime.

B. But isn't this very Saint Augustine of whom you speak the one writer of them all most given to playing with words? Do you defend him, too?

A. No, I won't defend him in that. That is the short-

[82] *De Doctrina Christiana,* 4.14.31.

coming of his time, the shortcoming towards which his lively and subtle mind gave him a natural bent. It is evidence that Saint Augustine was not the perfect orator; but it does not prevent him from having had along with it a great gift for persuasion. He is a man who reasons with singular force, who is full of noble thoughts, who knows the depths of the human heart, who is discreet and attentive in preserving in every discourse the strictest propriety —who expresses himself, in sum, with an almost invariable tenderness, warmth, and suggestiveness. Does not such a man deserve to be pardoned for the shortcoming we find in him?

C. It is true that I have never found one thing anywhere except in him, and I am going to mention it to you: he is moving, even though he uses conceits. No work has more of this thing than his *Confessions* and his *Soliloquies*. It must be granted that they are fervent and that they are capable of making the reader fervent.

A. That is because he tempers the conceit, as much as it can be, by the ingenuousness of his procedures and of his preferences. All his works bear the stamp of his love of God. Not only did he feel it, but he knew how to bring outward marvelously the sense which he had of it. In him you have the tenderness which makes up part of eloquence. Besides, we recognize that Saint Augustine knew the very heart of the true rules. He says that a discourse, to be persuasive, must be simple, natural; that its art must be concealed; and that, when it appears too elegant, it makes the listener distrustful. To it he applies[83] those words which you know: "What is uttered in falsehood deserves to be hated." With great knowledge he also discusses the arrangement of subject matter; the mixture of diverse styles; the ways to make a discourse forever grow; the necessity to be simple and familiar, even at times in the tones of the voice and in gestures, though what one says be elevated when one preaches of religion; and finally, the way to overpower and move.

[83] *De Doctrina Christiana*, 2.31.48. The quotation is from *Ecclesiasticus*, 37.23.

145

There you have Saint Augustine's conception of eloquence. But do you want to see how in practice he had the art of entering minds and how he sought to move the passions, according to the true end of rhetoric? Then read what he reports[84] himself of a speech he made to the people at Caesarea in Mauretania to get them to abolish a barbarous custom. He was dealing with an ancient custom which they had carried to the point of monstrous cruelty. I needn't say more. He was endeavoring to draw the people away from a spectacle which they found attractive. Judge for yourself the difficulty of that enterprise. Saint Augustine says that after he had spoken for some time, his listeners cried out and applauded him; but he decided that his speech would not persuade them as long as they were busy giving him praise. Of course he counted as nothing the pleasure and admiration of the listeners, and he did not begin to have hopes of success until he saw tears flow. "In effect," he adds, "the people gave up that spectacle, and for these eight years it has not been reinstated." Wasn't he there a true orator? Have we preachers who could do as much as that? Saint Jerome has likewise faults in style; but his utterances are virile and great. He does not hold to the rules; but he is much more eloquent than most men who take pride in holding to them. To study the Fathers only in respect to language and style would be to judge them as minor grammarians would. (You well know that eloquence must not be confused with elegance and purity of language.) Saint Ambrose also follows now and again the vogue of his times. He gives his discourses ornaments then much esteemed. It could even be that these great men, whose eyes were fixed on things loftier than the commonplace rules of eloquence, adjusted themselves to the taste of their times in order to make people listen with delight to the word of God, and in order to suggest the truths of religion. But after all, do we not find Saint Ambrose, notwithstanding some conceits, writing to Theodosius with an inimitable strength and persuasiveness? What tender-

[84] *De Doctrina Christiana*, 4.24.53.

146

ness does he not express when he speaks of the death of his brother Satyrus! We even have in the Roman breviary a discourse of his[85] upon the head of John the Baptist, whom Herod still respected and feared after his death. Study it— you will find the last part of it sublime. Saint Leo is bombastic, but he is great. Saint Gregory the Pope came at an even worse time; yet he wrote many things with great strength and dignity. We must know how to distinguish between what bad contemporary conditions led these great men, and all other writers of their times, to do in persuading their listeners, and what their own genius and feelings led them to do.

C. What? Is it true, as you would have it, that everything was decadent in respect to eloquence during the very centuries which were so favorable to religion?

A. Unquestionably. A short time after the reign of Augustus, eloquence and even the Latin language began to be corrupted. The Fathers arrived on the scene after this decline. Thus they must not be taken as safe models in everything. It must even be admitted that the larger part of the sermons we have from them are their least vigorous works. When I pointed out to you just now, by the testimony of the Fathers, that the Scripture is eloquent, I thought to myself that these were witnesses whose eloquence is quite inferior to that which you have accepted only upon their authority. There are men of so depraved a taste that they will not feel the beauties of Isaiah, but will admire Saint Peter Chrysologus, in whom, notwithstanding the fine name they have given him, one must look for the foundation of gospel piety underneath an infinitude of bad epigrams. In the Orient, the good way of speaking and writing was maintained longer. There the Greek tongue was preserved almost in purity. Saint Chrysostom spoke it very well. His style, as you know, is wordy; but he does not search for false ornaments—everything of his tends towards persuasion. He places each thing according to plan, he un-

---

[85] Ambrose, *De Virginibus*, 3.6, in J. P. Migne, *Patrologiae Latinae*, vol. 16, pp. 239-41.

derstands the sacred Scripture and the manners of men, he enters the heart, he makes things concrete, he has lofty and sound ideas, he is not without sparkle. Taking his work as a whole, you can call him a great orator. Saint Gregory of Nazianzus is more concise and poetic, but a little less concerned with persuasion. Still, he has some deeply moving passages; for example, his farewell to Constantinople, and his funeral oration for Saint Basil. Saint Basil himself is sober, sententious, even austere in diction. He had profoundly meditated upon every detail of the Gospels; he was deeply aware of the maladies of men, and is a great teacher of the government of the soul. One can find nothing more eloquent than his epistle to a fallen virgin—to my mind, it is a masterpiece.[86] If one does not have a taste formed from such things as these, he runs the risk of borrowing whatever is less good from the Fathers, and hence of bringing their faults together within the sermons which he composes.

C.   But that false eloquence which you spoke of as succeeding the true—how long did it last?

A.   Up till now.

C.   What! Up till now?

A.   Yes, up till now. And we are not yet rid of it, however much we believe we are. You will soon understand the reason why. The barbarians who overran the Roman Empire tended everywhere to show ignorance and bad taste. We are descended from them. And although literature may have begun to revive during the fifteenth century, its recovery has been slow. We have had trouble returning to the good way. And there are still many persons too far off to recognize it. We must continue to respect not only the Fathers but also the righteous authors who wrote during that long interval. In them we learn the tradition of their times and find many other highly useful teachings. I am quite ashamed to render a verdict on this matter. But you recall, sirs, that you wished it, and that I am entirely ready

---

[86] Basil, Letter 46; see Deferrari, *Saint Basil The Letters with an English Translation* (The Loeb Classical Library), vol. 1, pp. 282-311.

to retract, if you make me see that I am wrong. It is time to conclude our conversation.

C.   We aren't going to let you go until you have told us your opinion of the way to choose a text.

A.   You understand of course that texts originated from the custom preachers formerly had of never drawing upon their own ideas in speaking to the people. They sought only to explain the words of the text of the Scripture. Little by little they adopted the practice of not keeping to the exact readings of the Gospel; they did not explain anything beyond a single passage, which they called the text of the sermon. Therefore, if we do not give an exact interpretation of all parts of the Gospel, we must at least choose from it the words containing those truths that are most important and best suited to the needs of the people. We must explain them well; and in order to make the force of an utterance well understood, we must usually explain many others which precede and follow it. We ought not to search for subtleties in them. Oh that a man should have the bad grace to wish to appear inventive and ingenious, when he ought to be speaking with all the weight and authority of the Holy Spirit, whose words he borrows!

C.   I admit that forced texts have always displeased me. Have you not noticed that preachers rend from one text all the sermons they please? They twist their subject matter little by little in order to adjust the text to the sermon that they have need to spout. Such things happen particularly in Lent. I cannot approve of them.

B.   Don't stop, please, without having explained one further thing that gives me some difficulty. After that, I'll allow you to go.

A.   Oh well! Let's see if I can satisfy you. I have a strong desire to do so, for I devoutly hope that you will use your talents to preach simple and persuasive sermons.

B.   You would have a preacher explain the sacred Scripture consecutively and literally.

A.   Yes, that would be fine.

B.   But how does it happen then that the Fathers have

done otherwise? They always interpret according to the spiritual sense, it seems to me. Notice Saint Augustine, Saint Gregory, Saint Bernard—they find mysteries everywhere, and hardly ever explain the literal meaning.

A. The Jews of the time of Jesus Christ had become adept in mysterious and allegorical meanings. It seems that the Therapeutae, who lived principally at Alexandria, and whom Philo pictures as philosophical Jews, although Eusebius maintains them to be early Christians, were completely addicted to such interpretations of the Scripture. It is in that same city of Alexandria that allegories began to have a certain renown among the Christians. The first of the Fathers to depart from the literal interpretation was Origen. You know the stir which he caused in the church. At first, piety inspired these interpretations; they had something ingenious, pleasing, and constructive about them. Most of the Fathers, following the taste of the people of their time and apparently their own taste as well, used these interpretations freely; but they always had faithful recourse to the literal meaning, and to the prophetical, which is literal in its way, in all things where it was their concern to point out the foundation of doctrine. When the people had been perfectly instructed in whatever the literal meaning could teach them, the Fathers gave them those spiritual interpretations in order to enlighten and console them. These latter interpretations were entirely to the taste of the Orientals, above anyone else, with whom they had originated; for they are naturally enamoured of mysterious and allegorical language. This sort of meaning gave them concrete pleasure, because frequent sermons and almost continuous readings of the Scripture were matters of usage within the church. But among us, where the people are infinitely less well educated, preachers ought to take the shortest route and begin with the literal meaning; without cherishing any disrespect, of course, for the spiritual meanings given by the Fathers. One must have bread before he has spice. So far as the interpretation of the Scripture is concerned, one cannot do better than imitate the good example of Saint Chrysostom. Most of the men of our time do not seek after allegorical interpretations because they have already explained sufficiently each literal meaning; rather, they abandon the literal meaning because they do not see its grandeur and because they find it dry and unproductive in relation to their style of preaching. One finds all truths and every particular of morality within the literal meaning of the sacred Scripture; and one finds these things there possessed not only of a marvelous authority and beauty, but also of an inexhaustible abundance. In holding himself to them, a preacher will never have trouble in finding a large number of new and lofty things to say. It is a deplorable evil to see how much this treasure is neglected even by those who have it every day within their grasp. If we held fast to the ancient method of composing homilies, we would have two kinds of preachers. The ones, having neither liveliness nor poetical genius, would explain the Scripture in simple terms without adopting a lofty and living style. If only they did so in a sound and exemplary way, they would not fail to be excellent preachers; they would have what Saint Ambrose requires: a diction pure, simple, clear, full of weight and sobriety, without a pretense of elegance, and without a distrust of smoothness and harmony. The others, having poetical genius, would explain the Scripture in the very style and image of the Scripture, and thus would be perfect preachers. The former would teach in a strong and venerable way; the latter would add to strength of teaching that sublimity, that enthusiasm, and that vehemence of the Scripture, to the end that it would become, so to speak, as completely whole and living in them as it can be in men not miraculously inspired from above.

B. Oh sir, I forgot an important point. Wait, I beg of you. I ask you for no more than a word.

A. Must we again criticize someone?

B. Yes, the panegyrists. Don't you believe that, when one eulogizes a saint, he must portray his character by reducing all his deeds and all his virtues to a single point?

A. That would serve to display the contriving and the subtlety of the orator.

B. I understand. You do not relish that method.

A. It seems to me to be wrong for most subjects. It forces materials when they are all reduced to a single point. There are a great many deeds in a man's life, and they come from diverse principles and exhibit quite different qualities. It is a scholastic subtlety, and an indication that an orator is a long way from understanding nature, to have him want to attribute everything to one cause. The real way to make a portrait that will be a genuine likeness is to paint the whole man. He must be put before the eyes of the listeners precisely as he speaks and acts. In describing the course of his life, one must place principal emphasis upon those events where his character and his charm appear the more fully; but one must dispense with a few of these things in indicating them to the listener. The best way to praise a saint is to recount his praiseworthy deeds. There you have what gives body and force to a eulogy; there you have what teaches; there you have what moves. The listeners often go away without knowing the life of the saint whom they have heard discussed for an hour. At best they have heard many observations upon a small number of facts detached and emphasized without connection. You should on the contrary portray the saint in his own character, show him as he was in every period, under all conditions, and in all the principal junctures, through which he passed. That will not prevent you from calling attention to his character— you will even call attention to it much better through his deeds and his words than through the thoughts and designs of your imagination.

B. You would want one then to give the story of the life of the saint, not his eulogy.

A. Pardon me, but I would not give a simple story. I would be satisfied with giving a pattern of the principal events; but I would want this to be a story that was concise, rapid, living, full of variety. I would want each word to give a lofty idea of the saints, and to be a lesson for the listener. To this I would add all the moral observations which I thought most fitting. Don't you believe that a discourse made in this fashion would have a lofty and agreeable simplicity? Don't you think that the lives of the saints would become better known by such means, and that the people would be more enlightened? Don't you even suspect that, according to the rules of eloquence as we have laid them out, such a discourse would be more eloquent than all those stilted eulogies that you ordinarily hear?

B. Now I can well understand that such sermons would be not less instructive, not less moving, not less agreeable than the others. I am satisfied, sir. That's enough. It is right that you should go rest. As for me, I hope that your labors will not be wasted; for I have resolved to abandon all the modern miscellanies, and all the Italian *pensieri*. I want to study quite seriously all the interconnections and all the principles of religion in its sources.

C. Farewell, sir. In all gratitude, I assure you that I shall accept your views.

A. Good evening, gentlemen. I leave you with these words of Saint Jerome to Nepotian.[87] "When you teach in the church, do not stir up applause; stir up lamentations in the people. Let the tears of your listeners be your praise. The discourses of a preacher must be full of the sacred Scripture. Don't be a declaimer, but a true teacher of the mysteries of your God."

[87] Jerome, Letter 52; see Wright, *Select Letters of St. Jerome with an English Translation* (The Loeb Classical Library), pp. 188-229, especially p. 211.

Index

Except for the few special items indicated below, references to Fénelon are not indexed. References to eloquence are indexed only to indicate key passages in which the term occurs in these pages.

Aaron, 121, 127
Absalom, 60
Achilles, 74, 75
acting, 84
Aeneas, 74, 75, 93
Agricola, Rudolph, 11
allegorical meaning, 149-151
Amantius, Bartholomaeus, *Polyanthea*, 86
Ambrose (St.), 146, 151; *De Virginibus*, 147
Ante-Nicene Christian Library, 137
Antonius, 3, 97
Antony, 91
Apostolical Constitutions, 137
Aquilius, 97
Archimedes, 16
architecture, 2, 117-118
Aristotle, 1, 5, 8, 12, 16, 23, 26, 29, 45, 117; *Categories*, 13, 14; *Metaphysics*, 13, 14; *Physics*, 13, 14; *Poetics*, 71; *Rhetoric*, 11, 14, 44, 64; *Topics*, 10, 11, 14
Arnauld, Antoine, 6, 7, 25-33, 35, 36, 37, 42, 43, 45; *Art of Thinking*, 33; *Logique de Port-Royal*, 26; *Logique ou l'art de penser*, 26; *Port Royal Logic*, 26-32, 35, 36, 37, 41, 42
arrangement, *see* disposition
Artemisia, 58, 60
Ash Wednesday sermon, 4, 40, 43, 57-61, 98, 99
Athens, 69
Augustine (St.), 6, 26, 44, 45, 72, 123, 124, 127, 136, 138, 139, 140, 144, 145, 146, 150; *Confessions*, 123, 145; *De Catechizandis Rudibus*, 142; *De Doctrina Christiana*,

1, 45, 72, 91, 92, 124, 138, 139, 144, 145, 146; *Soliloquies*, 145
Augustus, 147
Aurelian, 64

Bacon, Francis, *Advancement of Learning*, 16, 24, 25; *De Dignitate et Augmentis Scientiarum*, 16, 25
Baker, Thomas, 52
Baldwin, C. S., *Medieval Rhetoric and Poetic*, 45
Barnard, H. C., *Little Schools of Port-Royal*, 33, 35
Bartlett, John, *Familiar Quotations*, 86
Basil (St.), 137, 148; *Address to Young Men on Reading Greek Literature*, 137
Bausset, L. F., *Histoire de Fénelon*, 36
Belshazzar, 131
Bernard (St.), 52, 112, 150
Beurhusius, F., 11
Bible, 2, 3, 5, 59, 60, 119, 120, 121, 122, 123, 124, 128, 130, 131, 132, 133, 134, 135, 136, 137, 138, 139, 141, 142, 147, 148, 149, 150, 151, 153; New Testament, 123, 133; Old Testament, 132, 133; King James Version, 58, 131; Vulgate, 58, 131; *Apocalypse*, 133; *Book of Wisdom*, 132; *1 Corinthians*, 122, 124, 128; *2 Corinthians*, 123; *Deuteronomy*, 131; *Ecclesiasticus*, 132, 145; *Genesis*, 60; *Isaiah*, 131; *John*, 132; *Maccabees*, 132; *Matthew*, 139; *Psalms*, 58, 59, 60, 101, 102, 131; *2 Timothy*, 140; *Titus*, 69
Biographie Universelle, Ancienne et Moderne, 18
Boileau, *Art of Poetry*, 2, 71; translator of Longinus, 64
Bossuet, 112; *Panégyrique de Saint Paul*, 112

155

INDEX

Bourdaloue, 99
Brinsley, John, *Ludus Literarius*, 20
Butler, Charles, *Rameae Rhetoricae Libri Duo*, 20; *Rhetoricae Libri Duo*, 20

Callicles, 78
Campagnac, E. T., 20
Campbell, George, *Lectures on Systematic Theology and Pulpit Eloquence*, 50
Carcassonne, E., *État présent des travaux sur Fénelon*, 36, 47; *Fénelon l'homme et l'œuvre*, 4
Caron, *see* Gosselin
Cherel, A., *Fénelon au xviiie siècle*, 46, 47
Christ, *see* Jesus
Chrysostom (St.), 136, 147, 151
Cicero, 1, 3, 6, 10, 12, 13, 17, 23, 29, 30, 41, 44, 45, 50, 62, 65, 76, 78, 82, 83, 85, 87, 89, 90, 91, 92, 94, 95, 96, 97, 102, 105, 109, 111, 112, 113, 123; *Brutus*, 97; *De Inventione*, 11, 44, 112; *De Oratore*, 3, 45, 76, 78, 83, 84, 87, 90, 91, 92, 95, 96, 97, 99, 102, 105, 107, 109, 112, 117, 130; Orator, 83, 84, 90, 91, 92, 97, 99, 102, 105, 108; *Topics*, 10, 11
Clauberg, 30
Clement (St.), *Pedagogue*, 142
Combéfis, François, 42, 86; *Bibliotheca patrum concionatoria*, 86
commonplaces, 13-14, 28-30, 35-36, 41-42, 45, 85
Congregation of the Oratory, 33
Cooper, Lane, *Plato*, 69
Corinth, 69
Coubé, M. l'Abbé, *Bourdaloue Orateur*, 99
Craig, H., *The Enchanted Glass*, 7
Crassus, 3
Crete, 69
Cyprian (St.), 144; *Epistle to Donatus*, 144
Cyrus, 118

dancing, 68
Daniel, 131

David, 60, 68, 127
Deferrari, R. J. and M. R. P. McGuire, *St. Basil the Letters*, 137, 148
Delaulne, Florentin, 46
delivery, 10, 11, 17, 19, 21, 22, 27, 34, 38-39, 42, 45, 96-105, 108, 109
Demosthenes, 2, 37, 38, 62, 63, 65, 97, 102, 109, 111
Descartes, 25, 26; *Discours de la Méthode*, 17, 26, 28
Despois, E., *Fénelon. Dialogues sur l'éloquence*, 53; *Discours de réception à L'Académie Française*, 53
dialectic, *see* logic
Dido, 93
Dionysius of Halicarnassus, 1, 2, 63, 109; *De Admiranda Vi Dicendi in Demosthene*, 63; *De Isocrate Iudicium* in *De Oratoribus Antiquis Commentarii*, 109
disposition, 10, 11, 12, 13, 14-16, 18, 22, 23, 24, 27, 28, 29, 35, 39-41, 42, 45, 58, 61, 111-114
division, *see* disposition
Donaldson, J., *see* Roberts, A.
Donatus, 144
Doyon, R.-L., 26
Duhamel, P. A., *The Logic and Rhetoric of Peter Ramus*, 9
Du Pac de Bellegarde, G. and J. Hautefage, *Œuvres de Messire Antoine Arnauld*, 26, 27, 28, 29, 30, 31, 32, 36, 42
Dupanloup, *Ministry of Preaching*, *see* Eales, Samuel J.

Eales, Samuel J., 49, 52; *Three Dialogues on Pulpit Eloquence*, 52; translator of St. Bernard, 52; editor of Dupanloup's *Ministry of Preaching*, 52
Ehninger, D., *Bernard Lami's L'Art de Parler: A Critical Analysis*, 35
Ellis, R. L., *see* Spedding, J.
eloquence, 61, 62, 68, 87, 90, 92, 95, 125-133; and acting, 84; and architecture, 117-118; and history, 84, 93; and logic, 30-32, 42, 45, 84, 89-92; and music, 68, 102, 114-115;

156

INDEX

and painting, 92, 93, 96, 119; and
philosophy, 84, 89-90; and poetry,
2, 3, 68, 84, 93-95
Estienne, Jacques, 46
Euripides, 71; *Philoctetes*, 117
Eusebius, 150
Eustochium, 123

Fathers, 3, 138-139, 143-148, 150-151
Fénelon, *Discours de réception à
L'Académie Française*, 53; *Lettre
sur les occupations de L'Académie
Française*, 45, 46, 49-50, 112
Fénelon's grandnephew, *see* Marquis
of Fénelon
Fenner, Dudley, 21, 22; *Artes of
Logike and Rethorike*, 22
figures, *see* tropes and figures
Fléchier, Esprit, 98, 99
Fludd, 26
Fouquelin, Antoine, *La Rhétorique
Françoise*, 18
Fraunce, Abraham, *Arcadian Rhet-
orike*, 21; *Lawiers Logike*, 22

Gassendi, P., *Institutio Logica*, 26,
27; *Opera Omnia*, 27
geometers, 89
gesture, 19, 21, 38-39, 84, 97-105
Glanvill, J., 43, 44; *Essay concern-
ing Preaching*, 43; *Seasonable De-
fense of Preaching*, 44
Godbid, W., 33
Gorgias, 78
Gospels, *see* Bible
Gosselin and Caron, 47
Gracchus, 96
Graeculi, 130
grammar, 27
Graves, F. P., *Peter Ramus*, 7, 9,
11, 22
Gregory the Great (St.), 150
Gregory of Nazianzus (St.), 150
Gregory the Pope (St.), 147
Griselle, E., *Bourdaloue histoire
critique de sa prédication*, 99

Hamilton, Adams, and Co., 51
Hautefage, J., *see* Du Pac de Bellegarde, G.

Heath, D. D., *see* Spedding, J.
Helen, 115, 116
Herod, 147
history, 84, 93
Hobbes, Thomas, 26
Holy Ghost, 60
Holy Spirit, 130, 149
Homer, 68, 69, 95, 115, 119, 123,
130, 131; *Iliad*, 2, 74; *Odyssey*, 74-
75
Hoole, Charles, *New Discovery of
the old Art of Teaching Schoole*,
20
Horace, *Odes*, 69
Howell, W. S., *Rhetoric of Alcuin
and Charlemagne*, 11

invention, 10, 11, 12, 13-14, 18, 22,
23, 24, 27, 28, 29, 35, 36, 41, 42,
82-87, 137-142
Ionians, 69
Isaiah, 51, 131, 147
Isocrates, 2, 5, 6, 37, 38, 62, 63, 64,
65, 78, 98, 109, 111, 115, 116;
eulogy on Helen, 115-116; *Panegyric*, 38, 63

James Nisbet and Co., 51
James (St.), 130
Janet, P., 4; *Fénelon*, 4
Jansenism, 26
Jansenists, 37
Jenour, Alfred, 49, 51, 52; *Hints on
Preaching: Being Fénelon's Dia-
logues on Eloquence*, 51; *Com-
mentary on Isaiah*, 51
Jeremiah, 131
Jerome (St.), 123, 124, 146, 153;
letter to Eustochium, 123; to Nep-
otian, 153; to Paulinus, 124
Jesus, 5, 60, 122, 124, 125, 127, 128,
129, 130, 132, 150
John (St.), 130, 132
John the Baptist, 147
Johnson, T. H., *see* Miller, P.
Joshua, 127
Jude (St.), 130
Juno, 116

157

INDEX

Stevenson, William, *Dialogues concerning Eloquence,* 49-51, 52, 98, 99

Sturm, Johannes, 11, 24

style, 10, 11, 17, 19-21, 22, 24, 27, 31, 34, 37-38, 42, 57-59, 60, 61, 90-92, 96-97, 103, 107, 114-118, 130-133, 138-139, 143-148

Sylvius, Franciscus, 86; *Polyanthea,* 86

Talaeus, Audomarus, 7, 18, 19, 20, 21, 22, 23, 24, 25, 33, 34, 37, 38, 42, 43, 92; *Institutiones Oratoriae,* 18; *Praefationes, Epistolae, Orationes,* 8, 11, 18, 19, 22; *Rhetorica,* 18-21

Talon, Omer, *see* Talaeus

Tertullian, 143

text, choice of, 149

Themistocles, 79

Theodosius, 146

Therapeutae, 150

Theseus, 116

Thomson, T. D., 51

topics, *see* commonplaces

Tortius, Franciscus, 86; *Polyanthea,* 86

Trajan, 74

tropes and figures, 19-21, 24, 25, 31, 34, 37-38, 45, 58, 61, 63, 90-92, 101,

108, 109, 114-118, 130-133, 143-148

Tuve, R., *Elizabethan and Metaphysical Imagery,* 7

Ulysses, 74

University of Michigan Contributions in Modern Philology, 7

University Research Committee of Princeton University, ix

Valerius, 136

Venus, 116

versification and poetry, 94

Virgil, 29; *Aeneid,* 2, 29, 36, 74, 75, 93, 95, 118-119

voice, 19, 21, 38-39, 84, 97-105

Waddington, C., *Ramus,* 7, 9, 11, 12, 17, 18, 20, 22, 26

Waddington-Kastus, C., *De Petri Rami vita, scriptis, philosophia,* 17

Wade, Ira O., ix

Walthoe, J., 50

Wood, T., 50

Wright, F. A., *Select Letters of St. Jerome,* 123, 153

Xenophon, 118, 130; *Cyropaedia,* 118

Zenobia, 64

160